START
- to WIN

by

DAVID HANNON

© David Hannon 1994

ISBN: 0 9523310 0 4

Published by D. P. Enterprises Limited

Printed by The Universities Press (Belfast) Limited

Contents

Preface

The great majority of motivational books are written in an American setting and designed for an American readership. As a result many of the illustrative stories used can lose some of their impact on a European reader.

In setting out to write 'Start - to Win' the author wishes to acknowledge a great debt to many of those American authors whose inspirational work has helped him in the preparation of his own book.

The Author

When you pick up this book and read the Title 'Start - to Win' you may well ask yourself "Who is this man David Hannon and why has he written this book?" So I thought it would be a good plan to fill in some of the details and answer the question.

I was lucky enough to be born into a large and loving family. My father was a Church of Ireland clergyman of some standing and my mother's father was Managing Director of a Company of Clyde-based Scottish shipbuilders who married into a long-established family of North Antrim landowners.

Number three in a family of five brothers and one sister, like all the others I had the benefit of a good private education and the joy and delight of four years at Keble College, Oxford shortly after the end of World War II.

It isn't immodest to say that I was blessed with a good brain. Class work and study came easy. But perhaps the truth is that it came too easy - for I gradually became lazy and rudderless. I drifted without any specific plan and certainly failed to make the best of my opportunities.

It's hard to imagine in today's tough competitive world but when I left Oxford with my degree in Physics - a degree which was only remarkable because fewer people end up with Fourth Class Honours than with Firsts! - I had no idea what I was going to do with my life apart from a rather vague idea that I might be interested in teaching and there was a distant fascination in the developing world of broadcasting.

As luck would have it I met a good friend who was Headmaster of the school I had attended in my own early years.
"What are you doing with yourself?"
"No special idea."
"Would you like to come and teach? I'm looking for someone."
- That's how easy it was.
Seven years later, again - although this time at least in open competition - I fell into a job with the BBC as a Television Producer. Once again in the light of today's battles for jobs it is hard to imagine the BBC appointing a schoolmaster who had never seen a TV camera to such a job, but they did and I think it would be fair to say that I didn't let them down.

For the next seven years I enjoyed fascinating experiences covering events all over Northern Ireland with Outside Broadcast cameras. Everything from Rugby matches to State Occasions, from Light Entertainment shows based on Irish traditional music to Requiem Mass for a Cardinal, from Songs of Praise by the special choir established for the World Conference of Christian Endeavour to the memorable day when Ireland beat the West Indies at Cricket!

However by this time ambitions were beginning to stir and I began to raise my sights and look for new worlds. I was appointed BBC Head of Programmes in Belfast just after the outbreak of the Troubles which began in October 1967 and which have rumbled on ever since.

After two years in that job I decided to try to widen my experience outside the confines of Northern Ireland and I took up a two year secondment to Malawi in Central Africa as Director General of the national Broadcasting Corporation.

Here was a challenge. An organisation existed. That much was certain. But it had no structure and bounced along from day to day without targets, without evident leadership and all the time looking over its shoulder at its political paymasters for fear of putting a foot wrong or saying the wrong words at the wrong moment.

Comparing the situation for broadcasters in a developing country with that in one of the Western Democracies is an interesting exercise. European Broadcasters will go on at length about freedom and independence - a matter I will return to later in this book. They cannot understand that priorities in a small poor African country can be different.

I had no doubt on the matter myself. Here I was in an almost brand new Republic which celebrated its fifth anniversary while I was there and I was quite certain that my job was to help where I could in the nation-building that was going on all around me.

I also had to try to instil in the minds of the broadcasters I was training that they should have questioning minds - not for the sake of knocking the National Plan, rather for establishing the honesty and certainty of what they were saying.

Nowadays in our Western World it is fashionable as it was then to criticise the President of Malawi Dr Banda as a dictator. Perhaps he was - he certainly liked to have his own way. But whatever else he may have been he was a man with a certainty of vision, a man with a goal, a man who was determined that his small country would be able to stand on its own feet.

To achieve this he knew he would need men and women of calibre to run the country and he would challenge anyone who he saw fall short of the standards he knew were needed. "What a stupid question!" I have heard him say to a reporter who was being too respectful.

When you read the supercilious criticism of countries like Kenya, Malawi, Zambia and Zimbabwe it is all too easy to forget that in Kenya, for example, Jomo Kenyatta who was the first and much respected President was in fact born before the British took over that piece of Africa as part of the British Empire, that he lived throughout its entire time as a colony and that after leading the fight for independence he presided over its emerging years as a new and fledgling nation. All that in one man's lifetime.

How do we in the West have the gall to criticise the things that go wrong? The self-righteous arrogance to blame the new leaders for self-interest or tribalism? Who were the examples of leadership they had watched in action during the first fifty years of the 20th Century?

Who ran the territories as their own? Who exploited the natural riches and the massed native manpower for their own benefit? Who fought their own internecine European wars over the foreign fields of Africa? Who expected loyalty and life from Africans in arms in other parts of the world?

Who locked away the very men who eventually emerged as leaders because they found them trouble makers? Surely the very same people who today are so fiercely critical when they see the new African leaders employ so many of the same methods of rulership in their turn.

But enough of that. The purpose of this book is not to produce an essay on emergent Africa even though some of the points raised by these questions have real parallels in the way we ourselves run our own lives and manage our own relationships.

At least I achieved one particular target. I had a goal. My contract in Malawi was for two years, in which time I had to create a structure for the business and train my designated Malawian successor to be ready to step into my shoes. Two years later to the day I left the country confident that I had achieved those aims.

When I came back to Britain I moved into Local Radio Broadcasting - once again at the mercy of other people's whims. Certainly for a time I was not in control of my own destiny. For two years I was Manager of BBC Radio Leicester and then without any deliberate intent I was invited to become the first Managing Director of Downtown Radio - Northern Ireland's first and most successful Independent Commercial Local Radio Station.

Here was a fascinating challenge. A green field site and a staff to begin with of a Chief Engineer and myself. I believe that this was the first time in my life where I personally defined a goal which I was determined to reach.

In those early days in mid -1975 the most frequent question was "When will the station go on air?". Even when there was nothing to be seen but the bare bones of an office building without windows or doors, my answer was "If we are not broadcasting by St Patrick's Day 1976, I will be very disappointed." Just eight and a half months to design and build a sophisticated studio complex, to recruit and train a complete staff, to establish a commercial department and sell the advertising! No small goal!

But the discipline of the combination of a goal and a deadline can work near miracles. On March 16th 1976, with exactly one day to spare, we took off - and straight into an outstanding success story.

Within six months the new station had the biggest listenership in the region surpassing all the competing stations even including the BBC's most popular channel by 50%.[1]

As a broadcasting station Downtown was an instant success and as a commercial venture its performance exceeded its founders' projections. But as often happens there are times when even successful faces don't fit as I discovered in my own relationship with the Board of Directors. We didn't see eye to eye over the priorities which should rule the running of a commercial radio station and after three successful broadcasting years I was out of a job.

Talk of shock to my self-esteem. All my life I had landed firmly on my feet. Apart from a short hiatus after the return from Malawi there had always been no shortage of opportunity. Good jobs were offered. People had come looking for me.

Now although to my mind I was still the same man with the same talents and abilities and with a wide experience to offer, no one wanted to know. I applied for job after job for which I knew I

---

[1] Independent Audience Research figures for September 1976 showed Downtown Radio with a weekly reach of 76% as against 49% for Radio One.

was well qualified - but no joy was to be had. Basically the same question came time after time "Why did you leave Downtown?" Even though my answer was honest and as accurate as I could make it the question itself was an insuperable obstacle.

So there I was aged 48, with wife and three super children to support, unable to get a job.

And here I am going to interrupt the story to say a heartfelt "Thank you" to Joan the most loyal and loving wife, to Patrick, to Elizabeth Anne and to Tony for the marvellous support they gave me through those years. Years I may say of blow after blow to self-esteem when I had to begin to face the fact that perhaps I wasn't the answer to everyone's prayers!

One day I decided that enough was enough of trying to find someone else who would 'give me a job'. What other talents had I which I might develop? A very unusual answer came up.

During the years at Downtown I had taken personal responsibility for the station's Religious Programmes including a short three minute spot late night each evening. Under the title 'By Your Side' I had read a passage of scripture and given a short prayer. Believe it or not I had even developed a small but attentive personal fan club!

At about this time I also heard of Alex McCowan's remarkable one-man show in which he presented the whole of St Mark's Gospel from memory on stage. Here was an idea. Without his professional dramatic training I did not believe that I could memorise the whole book, but I did prepare the text with great care and I began to earn my living by giving Dramatic Bible Readings. Either the whole of St Mark or a shorter one-hour programme made up of David and Goliath, Naaman's Leprosy and the Passion Story from St Mark.

The short programme was designed for schools and for some six months I toured Northern Ireland giving as many as three performances a day. Even with the small fees which schools can afford this paid the bills and the fact of working restored my self-esteem.

Incidentally don't let people tell you that the old-fashioned English of the Authorised Version is too difficult for today's children. I have seen as many as a hundred five, six and seven year olds sit spell-bound as the stories unfolded - and not just the blood and guts adventure of David and Goliath, but right through the whole performance.

Performance has its rewards. After she had listened to my reading of St Mark, I was approached by a young University student who said "You know, I never thought about it before, but Jesus must have been a very difficult man to live with!" On another occasion a young Presbyterian minister came to me and said "I am suddenly ashamed of the fact that I spend hours thinking out and preparing my own sermons, but I never realised that I should also be spending a lot more time on the preparation of my readings from the Bible!"

Whether or not the Lord was waiting for me to get up off my seat where I was waiting for something to happen I don't know. But it is a fact that just as I was wondering what I would do for a living during the long summer months when no school audiences would be available, I was invited to take on a special job for Ulster Television in Belfast and I stayed with them until my 60th birthday brought involuntary retirement.

Since then I have worked as a consultant for various clients - some in broadcasting, some in marketing, and one (the one who encouraged me to write this book) an outstanding example of what a man can achieve who sees an opportunity to take his own future into his own hands and who has acted on that vision.

As a consultant I am self-employed and one thing has become more and more apparent to me as I have worked in this way. John Paul Getty was right when he set out his six points for success in business.

1. Be in business for yourself
2. Offer a product for which there is a need
3. Guarantee your product or service
4. **Give better service than the opposition**
5. Reward people who work for you
6. Build your success on the successes of others.

All six of these points certainly apply to me in my business - and I don't mind underlining No 4, because one thing I know is that if the service I offer isn't better than the competition then I am out of business!

It was about ten years ago that I first came across the vast library of motivational books and one thing about them that has struck me is that they have nearly all been written by Americans. That does not surprise me too much because I believe that America has for years been a land of great opportunity and so it is natural that people there have made a study of the techniques of success.

Many of the books are inspiring and will give the reader a strong lead and a clear signpost along the road to successful self-improvement.

All the same the idea has been put to me that there is room for another book where the illustrations and examples used are drawn from our own experience here in Britain or from the activities and achievements of internationally recognised figures.

Out of many books on offer one with a clear message which I have used as a guide-line in writing 'Start - to Win' is 'The Winner's Edge' by Dr Denis Waitley and I hope that he will accept this acknowledgment of his inspiration as the thanks and tribute it is meant to be.

The book that follows is dedicated to my wife Joan without whose constant support I would not be in a position to write it.

Introduction

Some Men are Born Great
Some Achieve Greatness
And some have Greatness thrust upon them.

Shakespeare

This famous quotation underlines a simple but basic truth. The fact that there are three ways of reaching greatness.

1. By birth and background
2. By self-determination and your own efforts
3. Almost by accident because no one else will take on the responsibilities.

In many ways the same saying could be applied to leadership. Some men are born leaders. Some men make themselves leaders and some men have leadership thrust upon them.

In any society it is easy to see that about five percent of the people lead and the other 95% follow. Or to put it another way 5% are 'winners' and it's the winners who do the leading and gain the rewards and satisfaction of achievement.

So then the question is who are going to be the winners? Who are going to be the leaders? Who are going to be the achievers?

For many years the idea of **winning** has always carried the opposite side of the coin - the idea of **losing.** For someone to **win** it was necessary to have someone who **lost.** But is this the answer to the question - what do you want to do with your life? It doesn't have to be so.

There are many different ways of getting to the top. Basically they boil down to two. One in which your route to the top is littered with the bodies, lives and careers of all those you climbed over and trampled down on your way. The problem with that way is that when you get to the top it suddenly becomes a very lonely place and if you listen carefully what you can hear is the sounds of the next person following the very route you took and pausing now and then only to dig away at the foundations on which you own position is based.

The other winning way is to build your success by helping others to be successful. As you make your way towards the top lean down to help those who are with you. Offer them a helping hand and for sure in turn you will feel the lift and support from below as you face the next step upwards.

One man can climb a mountain on his own but if he slips or falls it's a long way to the bottom and there is nothing to stop him. With a team effort, the same mountain face can be conquered just as certainly but with the knowledge that if one of the team loses a footing there are others at the end of the rope who will take the strain and halt the headlong tumble to disaster.

No one sets out to be a failure, yet very few can look back and say with any certainty "I am a winner".

What makes a winner?

In olden days this was a simple question with a simple answer. The knight who knocked down all the other knights in the tournament. The King whose armies won the battles. These were winners and they gloried in the philosophy"Might is Right".

As civilisations developed, great thinkers, writers, inventors, composers, philosophers, all emerged and were recognised. These were men and women of great intellect or special talent who achieved distinction and were admired for their achievements.

Such special people still abound today in ever widening fields. Perhaps in human terms the knights of old have been replaced by sportsmen and women. Certainly all over the world there is instant recognition of names such as Pele, Steve Cram, Seb Coe and Steve Ovett, Mohammed Ali, Carl Lewis, Said Aouita, Boris Becker, Steffi Graff, Nick Faldo, an endless list - you can probably make out your own.

Modern communication by television and radio, by film and newspaper has revolutionised the world. Even the brief passing talents of pop singers can draw screaming crowds on world tours. Beatles, Rolling Stones, Beach Boys, Abba, Osmonds, all winners – some for a season, some for years.

With such an amazing variety of reasons for fame the time is right to ask how did they make it? Is there some common thread that anyone can pick up and follow? Some attitude that anyone can take and apply to themselves?

Not everyone can be a Pavarotti, a Margot Fonteyn, a Nelson Mandela, a Margaret Thatcher, an Einstein or a Karl Marx.

But all of these different people - sportsmen and women, performers and politicians, pop stars, scientists or revolutionaries had something in common.

They had the imagination to see their own potential and the dedication and determination to develop and fulfil it each in their own way. There lies the challenge to those of us today who would be winners.

Two classic examples of developing potential in their own fields are the achievements of Kriss Akabusi and Sally Gunnell.

Kriss Akabusi came up the hard way. He was raised in an orphanage and led a fairly unfocussed life until he joined the army. There he discovered his basic athletic talent and before long became one of a group of talented 400 metre runners in the U.K. Always a marvellous team competitor he was an essential part of the British 4 x 400 metres relay squad but he never achieved athletic greatness in the individual event.

Because he longed to be a winner, in 1986 he decided to take up the challenge of the 400 metres hurdles which has always had the reputation of being the 'man killer' amongst athletic events. Very soon he became British champion, Commonwealth champion and European champion and as captain of the British team his inspirational performances consistently gave the team a winning start in international team competitions. His individual performances climaxed when he shattered David Hemery's 24-year-old record as he won the European Championships in 1990.

As a winner his team performances were unmatched and who will forget his triumphant flashing smile as he carried the British relay baton past the USA in the final leg to take the Gold Medal at the 1991 World Championships in Tokyo.

Kriss himself is a man of dedicated personal faith. He puts the winner's attitude this way:

"Apart from God-given talent, the most obvious thing in becoming a winner is to have the essential ability to change the challenge to your own potential and not to be scared of taking the chance that the change involves".

Sally Gunnell made a similar decision. For years she had been Britain's best 100 metre hurdler holding the UK record at 12.82 secs and winning Commonwealth Gold in 1986. But the very top level of performance at World level constantly eluded her.

Once again however here we had someone who wanted to be the best. So in 1988 Sally switched to the 'killer' race - the 400 metre hurdles. After nearly 10 years of senior competition this was a major decision, but determination, talent and the desire to be a winner combined to take her to the very top.

By 1992 she had won Olympic Gold at the event and in 1993 she won the Gold Medal in the World Championships in a new World Record time.

International Sports Writers voted Sally International Woman Athlete of the Year in 1993.

Both Kriss and Sally demonstrate classic examples of people who weren't satisfied with a high personal level of performance already achieved. People who know there is greater potential within themselves and have the courage to take hold of their own futures identify a greater goal and put total commitment into the achieving of it.

In today's world the real winners will be those who take the time to look at themselves and ask themselves the question "What is my potential?" When the answer comes they each will have an image of what they can see for themselves. The next questions follow "Is that the best that I can do? Is that as far as I can go?" If the answers to these questions are "Yes" then the time for planning has come. How can we get to the target potential we have set?

Achieving personal targets will always have an impact on other people. In John Donne's words "No man is an island". If I change, other people will be affected for better or for worse. When setting goals it is therefore important to try to work out just what the impact on others will be. If it is likely to be negative then it is probable that our chosen goals have been too self-centred. When our chosen goals can be seen to be likely to have a positive effect on other people then they are worth pursuing.

There is little positive satisfaction to be achieved from the kind of success which has been achieved at other people's cost.

The right goals as they are achieved will give you an internal sense of satisfaction and a knowledge of having done something worthwhile. Because of their external impact they will have improved your own human relationships and in their wake they will bring an increase in your personal happiness.

It is important to distinguish between 'happiness' and 'self gratification'. You cannot pursue 'happiness' as an end in itself.

Money can't buy it. It can only be a natural by-product of other things. It grows from contentment, from positive relationships with others and above all from a knowledge of the achievement of your potential or even of the various clearly defined stages along the way to that ultimate target.

Try to grab at it and it will almost certainly fly away from your grasping fingers. Happiness is not a gift for the selfish or the self-centred.

So we can see that being a winner is the result of setting challenging personal goals, striving to achieve them through the way you live your life amongst those around you and doing it with the knowledge that if your image of yourself and what you may become is the right one then you can be confident that happiness will be a natural consequence of your efforts.

Knowledge of such a fact may seem a small thing, but absorbing that knowledge and putting it into practice can have a revolutionary effect on your life. You have only to look at dozens of examples of success to see how small are the margins that separate the winners from the also-rans.

The race won by inches, the championship won by a tie-break, the huge contract won by a sealed bid just a single percentage point below the competition. Those extra inches, those few points in the tie-break, that winning percentage point - all these are the little things that represent the difference between winning and losing or to put a more positive face on it the difference between being a 'winner' and being an 'also-ran'.

For us the challenge may not be for a championship or for a mammoth business deal. It is much more likely to be on a human scale. Then the knowledge of the way to be a winner can be the edge that you need to convert you from just another runner to a place in the winner's circle - the knowledge that will give you the Start you need to Win.

This is your chance in the words of Shakespeare to go out and make yourself great - make yourself a winner.

Strategic Planning

One essential fact is fundamental to becoming a winner. It is so obvious that it may seem unnecessary to have to say it. In spite of that I am sure that it is worth saying.

If you want to be a winner you are going to have to make that decision to be a winner in your own mind.

Without that determination you may set out to try this or that little bit of the plan for success and the little bit you try may help. But little bits will only help a little.

So take a deep breath and jump in at the deep end. Say it out loud. "I am going to be a winner." Say it out loud to yourself and listen to what you are saying. When you hear yourself speaking with conviction so that you yourself believe what you are hearing take the next deep breath and tell someone else - your wife, your husband, your closest friend. Whoever it is you choose to tell, let them see that you have nailed your colours to the mast.

This technique of sharing your goal, of letting others know your declared intention, is one of the strongest weapons in helping you to get there. You can use it for many different purposes. Whether it is the decision to stop smoking or to lose weight the support of others in sticking to your guns and reaching your target can make all the difference between success and failure.

Techniques can help - otherwise there would be no point in writing a book like this - but there is no magic wand. The motivation, determination and drive must come from inside. Of course attitude helps and the very first step along the winning road is to have developed the winning attitude.

The day (even the moment) when you declare "I am going to be a winner" and convince yourself that you mean it you have already reached your first goal. Believe it, it's true.

Going back to the words of the ancient wise man - the longest journey begins with a single step. So recognise the destination, the winner's circle. Realise that it can be quite a long way off but see too that there are clear steps along the way and plan to reach them.

Once you are on the road, once you have begun to follow the signposts to success, everytime you pass one of the milestones you have become a winner.

The first step, the all-important one, the declared intention first to yourself and then to others sets you on the way. When you take it you are on the road and you can already say in that small moment "I am a winner- I can do it."

When I go swimming I know that I am going to enjoy it. I love the water. And yet every time, I dip my toe in and say "It feels cold". Once I make the decision, once I take the plunge, I stay in the water for a long time - and the extraordinary thing is that if I go back to the shallows at the water's edge, the places that felt cold at the beginning when I was making the decision now feel warmer and quite comfortable.

So take the decision and come on in. The water really is warm where winners swim.

I have already mentioned the value of sharing your decision with others as being a powerful weapon in achieving your goal. Certainly if you associate with people you know are winners they will help you. Real winners are never jealous of their own success or selfish about sharing their attitudes. If you spend time with them their attitudes will rub off on you and you will find it easier to learn and practise them yourself. But remember other people can't do the job for you. Becoming a winner is your challenge, your decision and yours to achieve.

Other winners can show you the signposts, they can point you in the right direction, but each step along the road is one which you must take for yourself.

To make a success of becoming a winner you are going to have to take a really close look at yourself. To examine your life and the way you lead it and plan it under your own personal microscope.

Generally speaking no-one would normally recommend selfishness or self-interest as a virtue to be practised and neither do I. But at the same time it is important to underline that it is only by doing things for yourself (rather than expecting others to do them for you) and by setting standards for yourself that you are going to have any hope of achieving the potential that you are going to demand from yourself. That kind of **self**-ishness and **self**-interest is perfectly in line with even the most strict interpretation of moral and religious teaching if only because no plan for yourself will succeed unless it is built on the concept of good neighbourliness.

Remember to include "Do unto others as you would they should do unto you" in your philosophy and in your plan for your future, and your kind of **self**-ishness will make you welcome wherever you go.

Your success will be built on being honest with yourself, by building yourself into someone you can respect, by seeing the image of yourself as you know you ought to be able to be, by expecting achievement of yourself and by making sure that you add a new dimension to the yourself of the future.

Look at these standards and see what a difference each can make to you and the way you live your life.

1. Be honest with yourself and about yourself and apply that standard to your relationships with other people.

2. Look closely at yourself and make sure that what you see is a person you can respect.

3. Look ahead for yourself and build an image of what you plan to become. Identify the steps along the road to achieving that image.

4. As you make plans for yourself realise that the only limits on those plans are put there by your own expectations of what you may achieve. Be aware of the impact of how you assess yourself on your level of achievement.

5. Recognise that living the winner's life will add new dimensions to you and to those around you.

It might seem a contradiction in terms but you will achieve greatness very often if an essential part of your plan is built around the concept of making the other fellow great.

So the **Strategy** has been defined. The target is becoming clear in your mind. You are determined to make yourself a winner.

Strategy defines the ultimate purpose painted in broad brush strokes. It can only be achieved by the application of successful **Tactics** .

Tactics (1)

Be honest with yourself

What does that mean? First it means being able to step back and taking a good look at yourself as others see you - only remembering that you have an advantage over them in that you know what is behind the outer you. They can see the man or woman running a business, the salesman, the teacher, the girl who runs the efficient office, the husband who comes home to his wife, the wife who looks after the home and family. But can they see what's inside?

- the insecurity
- the jealousy
- the fiddled expense sheet
- the sense of guilt
- the frustration
- the pretence

If you are being honest with yourself you will be aware of your imperfections, your room for change and your potential as well as your limitations.

If you are going to be a winner you must also be honest enough to accept that it's up to you to take charge of your own future. It isn't going to be a matter of luck, or your stars, or fate or some other unlikely outside influence. Until you accept that fact, you will go with the prevailing wind - no longer master of your own destiny. If that's what you want, stop here and now and settle for second-best.

Wherever you are in life now, accept the fact that the future is in your hands. Where you are is your own responsibility - even if you want to pass on the blame to others - parents, bad luck, unsympathetic bosses, bad teachers, fate - whatever you want to call it. It's your life, you got to where you are, and you are going to take the decisions about where you go next. Of course you may get help, we can all do with it, but all the help in the world is no substitute for your own commitment, your own decision, your own determination to take on responsibility for your own future.

It's amazing how early in life you can begin to take your own decisions. My sister had a mind of her own from her very early days. At four years old she knew what she liked and what she didn't. She didn't like peas.

My mother was an equally strong character and she was brought up in the tradition that you ate what you were given and you didn't get the nicest things until you had dealt with the nasties! So in our family when there was ice-cream for Sunday lunch there was no ice-cream until all the vegetables had been eaten up.

My sister was given just five peas with the rest of her dinner. Everything was eaten except the peas. No ice-cream until the peas were gone. Eventually after a long struggle they disappeared. Ice-cream followed. What delight! Then the victory of childhood will. Once the ice-cream was finished my sister leant over her plate and carefully spat out the five peas!

Children learn early. What's more they learn how to control others, often including their parents. It doesn't take long for them to realise that crying, whining or tantrums soon attract attention or even to realise that Daddy is a softer touch than Mummy.

It is interesting to watch the interaction between small children and parents in public places like restaurants or aeroplanes. How often do you see the distraught almost panic-stricken look on a mother's face as a child goes into a routine of naughtiness.

The idea of discipline often seems to have vanished in today's world. New ideas have taken over and we have to learn how to live within their disciplines. Modern theory says no smacking, no corporal punishment, almost no blame. Maybe the ideas are right. But if they are we are going to have to find some other way to teach behaviour.

I am convinced that a young child is a happier child if it knows where it stands. If Mummy or Daddy has made it clear that this behaviour is acceptable and that is not, then the child can be secure. There is nothing wrong with a parent's vocabulary that contains a solid place for the simple word "No." There is something wrong with a world where people are so concerned with their **rights** that they forget their responsibilities.

After my early years in teaching I am horrified when I read today stories of parents attacking teachers who have tried to impose discipline on children. If you hope that your children will grow up as responsible members of society you must be sure that they learn that there are rules to be obeyed if life in the family, in school, or in the community is to be a success.

When I was a kid I knew the situation. If I was naughty I was punished. The policeman may have been a bit of a 'bogeyman' (How many mothers said "If you don't behave I'll get the police") but they were respected. Teachers ruled their classes with a cane or other discipline. All these things were accepted. No one ever told me that because I was only nine years old I didn't know when I was doing wrong. I did know- I can still remember!

What a contrast to the day when I caught three little boys in our vegetable garden wrecking all around them. I brought them into the kitchen and called the police (remember, I dare not touch them myself). As we waited two of the youngsters began to cry. They were aged about 7 and 4. Between them sat the third aged all of 6 years. He looked at them with contempt. "What are you crying for?" he said "He can't do anything to you!"

Is this the kind of society we want? I don't think so - and I'm sure that it is up to each of us to take on the responsibility for our own attitudes and the attitudes that will rub off on our children.

If they know that we lie and cheat, who is to blame if they put the same standards into practice in their own lives?

Be honest with yourself

So when we look at our own standards of behaviour who do we blame? Is it our parents' fault, our teachers' fault? Were we brought up in a setting that lacked the good things of life? To some degree the answer to some or all of these questions may be

"Yes" - but even if it is, that is no excuse for not trying to do something about it. The day that we decide to take responsibility for our own actions and our own attitudes is another day when we take a step along the winner's road.

From here on the decision is ours. We do things because **we decide to do them** not because **we have to do them.** In our modern society with its welfare provisions you can get away with doing nothing.

In our house we have a really attractive fully furnished 'granny-flat' where my wife's parents lived while they were still alive. Nowadays we rent it out. Among our most recent tenants were two girls both under 18 years old. They had no jobs and they both claimed that they had been put out of their family homes. Technically 'homeless', the state paid their rent. The sad thing is that if they went to work in average paid jobs for youngsters of that age they wouldn't have been able to afford the rent. Is that any sort of challenging existence for them? I wonder.

Generally speaking, people who only do things because others tell them that they must are not taking responsibility for their own lives. They get into the habit of letting things happen. Losers **let** things happen. Winners **make** them happen; they do something about the situation.

Constantly in the Bible - the classic all-time hand book - we come across the phrase **"Lift up your heads".** That is sound advice. When we lift up our heads high enough to see over the wall of circumstances that surrounds us we will have a broader vision. When we lift up our heads to see over the top of the nearby hill we can suddenly see the glories and the opportunities on the other side.

A challenge we have to face at every stage is to dare to be different. From our earliest years the pressures of other people's opinions exert tremendous influence. Look around and see the way in which young children insist on the right trainers or the same mountain-bike as everyone else. No matter if parents can afford them. Everything must be right. The pressure of the peer group has created the marketing man's dream world.

Looking back to my own childhood, I was lucky in the fact that my mother was strong-willed enough not to give in to every demand. My sister, my brothers and I as youngsters all rode about on what we called 'Rectory bikes'. Old second-hand machines that you could buy in those days for ten shillings, (50p in case you the reader are too young to remember!). The important thing was not that they were elegant but that they worked and got us where we wanted to go.

Looking at my own children I must be honest enough to say that we as parents felt the pressures of trying to be like the others. I only hope we reached a reasonable balance of meeting their needs without falling for every fad or fashion. And to be fair to them they were never too demanding.

When the teenage years arrive the natural instinct for children is to want to break free from parental control, to express individuality. But what happens? Have a look at any group of youngsters who go around together. Certainly the clothes may not be what parents would choose - but there they are all in sloppy joes, or grunge, or jeans or chinos or whatever the latest fashion is. Last year's fashion is just as deadly as a collar and tie. Later, as full adulthood beckons, the time arrives when we have to make our own complete decisions. Today the chorus cry is often 'Freedom'. Everyone wants the right to do their own thing. In the broadcasting world where I have spent many years I constantly come across men and women who are dedicated to the 'Freedom' concept. "No one tells me what to do!" is a common attitude.

Among journalists, what I have described as the unlimited arrogance of the dedicated liberal is one of the greatest problems. Read any paper - not just the raucous tabloids - listen to broadcast news bulletins and you will hear people being judged and criticised. Negative attitudes seem to sell papers and draw viewing audiences.

When I am invited to speak to groups of broadcasters I take the theme 'Freedom with Responsibility'. Not always popular! But I hammer away at the point that no one has the right to justify actions purely on the grounds of **Freedom** unless they are prepared to take responsibility for the consequences of what they have said or done. Even in this there sometimes seems to be no recognition of double standards. Public figures are pilloried for misdemeanours of morality, for public dishonesty, for dark personal secrets carefully unearthed. Very seldom does anyone ask "What are the standards being used by the critics in their own lives?".

In recent times it has been fascinating to watch the outcry by his colleagues when newscaster Martyn Lewis stood up and said what he believes. That there is too much bad news and that insufficient attention is paid to the positive side of life. He has noticed that if there is any sign of a television news bulletin running too long, the first items to be cut are the good news pieces.

He had the courage to say what he believes, and what happened? Long letters were written to the papers scorning his judgment. Journalists do not like being told that they are wrong. After all, in their own view, they are the professionals, so who is anyone else to disagree? The strange thing is they don't even seem prepared to go any distance along the line originally stated by Voltaire "I disapprove of what you say but I will defend to the death your right to say it".

Statistics show the vast number of hours that everyone spends in front of the TV screen. Surely it must be right to suggest that what people watch on screen, be they young or old, is going to have an effect on what they find acceptable in their own lives.

You will hear the argument that people know it's not real, that it's only entertainment or drama, that real life isn't like that so no-one will take any notice - and all this is said seriously with straight faces by people who are selling the breaks in the programmes to advertisers who are prepared to spend vast sums of money for the very reason that they **know** that constant repetition of a message will get it across.

As a small experiment ask yourself these questions and put down the first answer that comes into your head.

Are most policemen honest?

Are most prison officers decent people?

Is it all right for young people to live together before they are married?

Do you think that most men and women play around outside marriage?

At a guess most people will answer No, No, Yes, Yes because that is the normal situation painted on the TV screen. But stop a moment and think about it. Surely there is something wrong here.

Everyone accepts that police and prison officers are human beings and will have their failings, but in our society we cannot afford to accept that the wrong way is what we expect. The same applies to sex and marriage.

Only forty years ago I would have been quite happy to guarantee that the instant answers to my four questions would have been Yes, Yes, No, No. Can we afford to be complacent? Can we accept the judgment of those who are responsible for changing our attitudes? I don't believe so and I hope that as more and more people make the winner's decision for their own future they will have set standards for themselves and for the society they want to lead, which will be able to do something to change it.

The sad thing in all this is that the decline in our personal standards, in our moral standards, is taking place against a background of a world in which other standards are being revolutionised in the opposite direction.

Young athletes are matching yesteryear's world records, the miracle '4-minute mile' is commonplace. Wonder drugs are replacing operations. Laser operations are making surgery unnecessary. Organ transplants are giving back full lives to thousands. And yet the media tell us that the world lurches from crisis to crisis. From Ethiopia to the USSR, from Ireland to the Middle East.

There is a challenge to faith here. If we are honest enough to face up to the facts we will realise that our decisions at our own personal levels can be the beginning of a revolution in the attitudes within our own homes, within our own communities, within our own nations and ultimately within our world.

It is a revolutionary thought maybe, but it is a fact - that if a man or a woman makes a fundamental decision to change themselves the ripples of that decision will spread right across the whole lake of life of which they themselves form only a tiny drop.

* * * * *

Here are a few questions - and remember we are talking about honest answers

How much time do you spend with your children? If they are still living at home do you go out of your way to give each of them even five minutes of your special attention each day?

Can you talk fully and openly with them or do you too find the generation gap an insurmountable barrier?

Can you talk openly and honestly with your wife or your husband? Even if you can, let me give you a little piece of advice. Don't take your loving relationship for granted. Make a point of telling your partner in simple words "I love you" at least once every day.

I have already said that being a winner involves your relationships with other people, so doesn't it make tremendous sense to start with the relationship in which you are most closely involved every day of your life.

* * * * *

I remember a song that was popular in the 1940's and 1950's. Bing Crosby sang "You've got to accentuate the positive and eliminate the negative - don't mess with Mr In-between".

Much of today's world is built on negative words. The craze for Political Correctness sweeping America today may be a reaction to that situation in the way it tries to re-define situations that for years have been simply defined by single words like short, old, bald, deaf or whatever. As long as we use words in a straightforward way and not as dismissive or derogatory I cannot see the harm. However that's a subject for another day - maybe even for another book!

Does your life drive you or do you drive your life? Does this timetable sound echoes in the pattern of your daily round?

The Alarm Clock breaks into our sleep - whatever happened to cock-crow or sunrise.

*The Radio news to list what's **wrong** with the world today.*

*The Newspaper to tell us what was **wrong** with the world yesterday.*

*The struggle through commuters because **we have to go to work.***

The anger that surges against the stranger who cuts us up in the traffic.

The apprehension of opening the day's mail to find the bills.

The short breaks we have to take in the daily drudgery.

The cigarettes for the nerves - The quick drink to relax.

The gulped meal to make sure that we don't miss the latest episode in the TV soap with its 'real life' mixture of teenage sex, marital disaster, broken relationships, dishonest businessmen.

A hasty look at the clock to see if there's time to make it to tonight's neighbourhood meeting called to discuss the local outbreak of joy riding - and so to bed with the wife who asks "Had a good day, darling?"

Time for a sleeping pill!

Why won't people just leave me alone?

Do you recognise yourself? Is there something you can do to change the pattern? There is no need to accept the pattern where 'have to' has taken control of your life. Take a deep breath and step outside. You will find an ample supply of good fresh air outside the fusty living room of your daily pattern.

Remember as you look at yourself to see what the other people see. Give them the chance to change their opinion by pulling a few of the control levers governing your own behaviour. You will be surprised by the effect. When you make the decision you may well find that you are trying to unloose emotions that have been rusted solid by years of neglect. Don't be afraid - the rewards can be startling.

Maybe you have suffered for years from a terrible tension and distrust in your relationship with your mother-in-law. Thousands have. Indeed as the late Les Dawson used to tell us while we laughed in sympathy, a fraught relationship is par for the course.

So we come to deep breath time.

Go to the mother-in-law with a smile and thank her for the gift of her son or daughter - the gift that has added a whole new dimension to your life. And make sure you mean it when you say it. It can have an amazing effect!

That's only one example. Look at other relationships in your life. Ask yourself is there something I can do about the problems with the boss or with the difficult person who seems to cause all the trouble in your department or even quite simply with the colleague who shares your office.

You can be sure of one thing. If there are problems in any relationship they are never all one person's fault, so ask yourself what your contribution has been and what can you do about putting things right.

Is there jealousy, resentment, anger, unfairness or even simply defensiveness on your part? If there is, why not identify it, bring it out into the open and try the effect of the simple step of saying "I'm sorry". Remember "Sorry" means either "Sorry enough not to do it again" or "Sorry enough to do something about it". In the words of another song you will find that 'Sorry is a magic little word'.

The magic can arise from the change in the person who says it and means it or from the miraculous change it can produce in the person you say it to. Even though you may benefit from the results yourself there is nothing selfish about a genuine apology.

There are other ways of applying honesty to yourself. Take the question of *physical* honesty. Are you being honest in your dealings with your body?

Are you overweight? Are you gaunt and nervous? What kind of fuel are you feeding your miraculous human machine? Remember your body is the only one you've got!

Do you fill it with smoke? Do you put too much alcohol in the tank? Do you service its daily needs with junk food? Do you put it at risk by sexual self-indulgence or careless physical relationships? Do you take enough sleep to keep the batteries charged? This body of yours is a sophisticated machine that needs to be kept in the best possible working order.

In his book 'The Winner's Edge' Dr Denis Waitley describes an extraordinary experiment. He went to his bedroom and locked the door - or so he thought. Then he undressed and examined himself in a full-length mirror. Realising that when we look at ourselves in the mirror we nearly always concentrate on the familiar face gazing back at us, he covered his head with a paper bag with eye-holes cut in it. An honest appreciation of the nude stranger reduced him to uncontrollable laughter which only ended when his wife walked in through the 'locked' door.

There is a serious point behind the story. Too often we create an inaccurate picture in our own minds of what we really look like. So why not try Dr Waitley's experiment yourself. Once you have tried it check up on all the pills and potions you use to keep your body the way it is. Then ask yourself if that is the way you should be treating that essential and precious possession - your body.

If you are like most people you probably spend a lot of money on some personal self-indulgence. Give serious thought to using some of that money to making sure that you are being physically honest with yourself by planning for regular physical check-ups.

Incidentally when you do the Denis Waitley experiment, if you are shocked by the physical picture which you see in the mirror, try having an equally honest look at the other you - the person inside the body who does the thinking and makes the decisions. Then ask yourself are you happy with the standards you are setting for yourself. Are you happy with what you, **and only you,** can tell about what you are achieving?

* * * * *

People today often set out to seek some sort of artificial self-awareness. Enlightenment is the word used so often to justify experiments with drugs, LSD, biorhythms, the Moonies, meditation and so on. Some may bring passing benefit but passing is the word.

Earlier I said that happiness must be a by-product of a way of life - it cannot be an aim in itself. The constant restless pursuit of that fleeting butterfly is often the direct result of a lack of responsibility for managing our own behaviour in an effective way. The so-called search for enlightenment or for what we call our real selves may take years and after 20 years what would we find? Like as not the same old us, only 20 years older.

Each of us has a mind to use - and what an instrument it is. Think of all the things it can say to us in different situations. "He's lying" - "It's safe to overtake" - "I like you" - "I love you" - "I want to spend the rest of my life with you".

It's a remarkable computer with the extraordinary human dimension and don't forget the other thing it can say - "I can design and invent a bigger and better - or in today's world, a smaller and better computer".

Sure the computer can do miraculous things at remarkable speed and save years of mental time and effort. But so far no one has come up with one that can look at a situation and realise for itself that the time has come to be honest and say "I'm sorry".

Not long ago we were talking of physical honesty over the way we treat and maintain our bodies. We can take a parallel look at mental maintenance and the ways we look after our minds. Where do the limitations arise?

Laziness – "Why bother"

Fear – "It's too risky for me"

– and not only fear of failure but the fear of success which says that success is going to be beyond my grasp so it's not even worth beginning to try
or
the fear of success which worries about the responsibilities that success is bound to bring.

Attitude is the answer. In order to get into mental shape to match physical shape we are going to have to face up to a moment of truth. The moment that we make the commitment to move along the winner's path.

Everyone on earth has potential and if we say that all men are equal what we must realise is that they have an equal right to fulfil that potential whatever it may be, irrespective of colour, religious belief, sex, financial status, birth, intelligence, age or any other of the many concepts that seem to divide us.

To make our commitment we need a foundation on which to build. So set your standards - truth, integrity and honesty and remember that they apply to relationships within yourself and with others and to the management standards you set for body and mind.

Take control of your destiny. To become a winner, to reach your potential you must make your own decision and your own commitment. No one else can do it for you.

You will find it helpful if you make use of some of these ideas.

1) Look at your position in life honestly. Take the blame where you should but don't be afraid to take the credit where you deserve it.

2) Break into your set outline. Unplug the TV and use the time you have released for positive action.

3) Look at yourself through other people's eyes. What do your parents see? Your wife or husband? Your children? The people you work with?

4) Think about how others feel when you come in contact.

5) Look for truth. Don't automatically accept everything you hear just because its 'on the box' or in print.

6) Invest time and effort in developing your own knowledge and skills.

7) Take thirty minutes a day for yourself alone. Take the time to plan.

As Kipling puts it:

"If you can fill the unforgiving minute
With sixty seconds' worth of distance run
Yours is the Earth and everything that's in it
And - which is more - you'll be a Man my son"

As this chapter has been saying from the beginning

Be honest with yourself.

Tactics (2)

Be someone you can respect

Early on I have spoken of the two different ways of winning. There are those who win by climbing over everyone else on the way to the top and there are those who become winners as a result of helping other people to be winners too. When you become a winner make sure which kind you choose to be. Be someone you like!

In recent times we have all watched business after business taken over by the money men - the people to whom little about the business matters except the profit figure in the bottom right hand corner of the balance sheet. The soul seems to have vanished from the business process.

Until recent years commercial television used to be run by people whose primary interest was making programmes and having the best quality transmission pattern. There were commitments and relationships between those at the top and the rest of the staff. Of course there were problems. No business that is alive will ever be without them. Any organisation that has no tension and no stress soon becomes moribund and soon after that ends up as a corpse.

Nowadays in company after company the hard nosed money men have taken over control. In a determination to squeeze costs, long service staff are made redundant to be replaced by younger ones who will work at the bottom end of pay scales. In a very profitable business like commercial television it is depressing to watch trust and honour being sacrificed on the high altar of more profit.

Of course the Accountant is essential in any business. Everybody needs to know where their operation stands. Good accountants can help to make good decisions. But there is certainly a trend in the training available to accountants which points to the hard way - the single ruling philosophy of maximise revenue and minimise costs. Forget about people - they don't matter.

Look about you at any industry you know and you will see people with these attitudes taking more and more control. They see themselves as winners, they certainly are in command but who likes them? I wonder if they like themselves.

It isn't only in business. You can see the same thing in government where long term social commitments are being abandoned in an effort to 'Balance the books'. When Mrs Thatcher first became Prime Minister she had a prime target - to stop the country living beyond its means. That certainly made good sense and she achieved remarkable success.

As far as the Welfare State is concerned I do not wish to encourage a nation of people brought up to expect something for nothing. Such attitudes can only corrupt standards of personal morality. At the same time I am firmly committed to the idea that as a nation we must take responsibility for those in genuine need.

It is easy to see that there can be conflict between these two ideas. Trained economists cannot agree as to where the solution should lie. Wherever it is I do not believe that it should be achieved by breaking promises or shrugging off commitments that deserving people have been led to expect.

It may be facile to say "Tax the rich to help the poor" but it is true that unless the 'haves' are prepared to help the 'have nots' we must have chosen a selfish way.

* * * * *

Remember when you decide to be a winner that different people can do it at many different levels. You are not being challenged to be anything more than the best your potential has to offer.

In 1960 the Perry Como Show was one of the most popular musical TV shows available. The decision was taken to come to England and record a number of shows there. As the programmes were being partly financed by the BBC they supplied the cameras and most of the staff.

Ronnie, a friend of mine was BBC Stage Manager for the shows - not the most senior of positions. The Perry Como production team came over with the star to make sure the show worked in its usual highly successful way. Ronnie found himself working with his American opposite number and they were soon comparing notes.

The American Stage Manager pointed to the Director "I earn more than him!" he pointed to the Senior Cameraman "I earn more than him!" He was obviously one of the best paid people in the team. Ronnie asked him how this happened. "It's easy" said the American, "I'm the best durn Stage Manager in the business!"

Here was a winner, a man who knew his own worth.

Once you have stepped out on the winning road keep your thinking positive. Don't start looking for problems that aren't there. Avoid falling into the habits of remarks such as "Isn't the world in a terrible state" or "I don't imagine this good weather will last". There are far too many good things happening for us to let ourselves constantly get into habits of negative thoughts based on what might go wrong.

The creation of negative thinking habits can start at a very early age. All along I have stressed the importance of relationships with others as part of the winning programme. Think about your children and how you relate to them. When do they get your attention? Is it when they are being good or when they are being a nuisance? For most of us it is far too often when they are naughty or unhelpful or disobedient that they know they will be noticed.

What does that do for their own image of themselves? How will they begin to programme themselves to get your attention? It is easy to imagine the child saying however unconsciously "I only get Dad or Mum's attention when I'm bad - so if I want a lot of attention maybe I should do something really bad!"

Set out to build positive attitudes and responses in your children. From their earliest days you are the role model that they are bound to see most often. If you throw litter out of the car window as you drive along with the family don't be surprised if you find that the youngsters aren't interested in keeping their rooms tidy at home. Remember kids have ears and acute hearing and they seem specially skilled at hearing all the wrong things.

When my oldest brother was quite small the Bishop was coming to visit my father's Rectory. My mother warned my brother not to say anything about the visitor's appearance. Things went well until my brother came into the room where the Bishop was sitting to ask "When is the man with the funny nose coming?".

A simple enough story perhaps but an illustration of the simple innocence of children.

Watch little children of different colour play together. They just don't notice. It is we, the adults, who are responsible for introducing attitudes. Each of us is father or mother to the child. As we take on the responsibility of raising the family remember the other side of the coin. The child is father to the man.

So be open with the children. Make sure that your relationship isn't based on a series of "Don't do that" or "Stop that" commands. Answer questions as honestly as you can. A child who learns the facts of life lovingly explained by Mum or Dad is much less likely to get involved in teenage or even pre-teenage pregnancy or to go through life mired in guilt about sex as a result of hole in the corner experiments with something that seems to be 'Dirty'.

Children have an enormous talent for learning. Just think of the achievements of the early years. Walking, talking, the whole use of language. So at this absorbent stage of their lives we must be particularly careful of what we are teaching them by our actions and attitudes.

If children are constantly bombarded by criticisms from parents, from teachers or from other adults and if they are constantly exposed to the negative attitudes in the media where violence, immorality and dishonesty are the small change of everyday life, what can we expect them to learn?

Your attitudes will be clearly reflected in the mirrors of their lives. Positive love and affection and a fair share of your attention is a small price to pay for the happiness it will create. However worrying the latest row with the boss, or the rumours about job losses in the company or the latest disaster on the TV news, remember that for a small child the most important thing is to tell Mum and Dad what they did today and to know that you are listening. Make time for them today. Appreciate their achievements.

I was interviewing applicants for a job at Radio Leicester. Six were on the short list and judging by paper qualifications the outstanding candidate was an 18 year old girl whose A-level results were tremendous - Grade A in English, French and German and Grade B in Russian. I was greatly impressed but I thought I would take a light-hearted approach. With a smile, I asked "What happened to the Russian?". She started to cry.

It was of course all my fault. I had forgotten what the view would be from the other side of the interview desk. Instead of taking the positive attitude to her achievements, I seemed to her to be concentrating on what she felt had been a small disaster. It turned out that she had expected to get Grade A in everything!

Of course communication is a two-way process and it is important to remember to accept positive remarks made to you. A compliment is doubled in value if it is welcomed with an honest "Thank you". When the boss or the teacher or the parent says "Well done!" don't run away from your achievement.

When I was at school, for one summer term we were taught English by the Art Master the distinguished Irish sculptor Oisin Kelly. He was never very much driven by the normal disciplines of teaching and when reminded that Wednesday was the day scheduled for English home work he would say "Write an essay or a poem!".

At the age of fifteen I was just becoming aware of the world of politics and I sat down one evening and wrote nearly twenty pages of exercise book on what I thought should be done about the world's problems. When the books were returned to the class there was little in the way of comment or criticism in most of them, but when I opened mine there were six pages written in red ink taking up my arguments and responding to them.

What amounted to a correspondence between Mr Kelly and me developed all through the term. He may not have taught a lot to everybody in the class, but he had decided that my fledgling efforts demanded encouragement and his decision to communicate in depth has always stayed in my mind as a marvellous piece of teaching.

* * * * *

We live in a world where you hear a lot about equal opportunity, fair employment, discrimination and sexual harassment. I approve of the idea of making sure that the best person gets the job, man or woman, black or white, and in Ireland, where I live, Catholic or Protestant. At the same time I like to believe that men are men and women are women and there is more than just a physical difference.

I was brought up to open doors for women, to walk on the outside of my girl friend on the pavement, to restrain my language in the presence of women, to offer my seat on a crowded train. Most women appreciate such courtesies and I think it will be a great pity if the pressure for equality promoted by the most dedicated enthusiasts leads to a situation where they are resented in some way as the last vestiges of some kind of male chauvinism!

If a female colleague takes the trouble to dress smartly and to look well-groomed I like to be able to tell her that I have noticed. Even at my age if I make the effort to try on a new colour scheme or a new jacket I'm pleased if someone comments on it!

There are times when a little humility can be an amazingly effective weapon. I love playing bridge which is of course essentially about partnership. You will often find yourself at a table where the opponents spend all the time complaining and criticising their partner's mistakes. This cannot be a constructive attitude in the long run and the constant drip of complaint from your partner can corrode the trust of even the best partnership. I have found a very simple way of stopping the complaints from across the table which usually come in the form of questions like "Why didn't you play such and such a card?" or "Why didn't you do this or that?". I wait for a suitable pause and quietly answer "Because I'm not a good enough player".

Being a winner is a positive thing, yet it is amazing how people can resist the opportunity to change onto a winning path. Fear of change combines with fear of success, and people will go out of their way to set unrealistic goals so that when they fail to reach them they can have an excuse for not trying again.

Like the lady of the manor who read in her Bible "With faith you can move mountains". Outside the window of her bedroom a glorious view was blocked by a mountain.

So she prayed that the mountain would be moved. Next morning when her maid came into the room to open the curtains the lady asked "Mary, is the mountain still there?". "It is indeed, my lady" replied the maid. "I knew it would be" said the lady.

A simple tale perhaps but with a hint of an important truth in it.

Be realistic when you set your targets. Apart from the fundamental change brought about when you decide to take the winner's path, understand that it is likely to be a long road to travel if only because every time you reach what might look like the far end you will find a new view around the corner.

* * * * *

People who don't have proper respect for themselves, whose self-esteem is low have different ways of showing it.

Loud-mouthed braggart juvenile delinquents are often totally insecure inside. Experience has taught them not to trust relationships with others and so they shout their independence and their contempt for authority. It's not only juvenile delinquents who suffer in this way. You may find someone who should be close to you has shut a mental door in your face. Knock gently on it and try to encourage the frightened body to come out and meet you again.

Sometimes relationships can be damaged by quite little things like social slights. Very often the person who has caused the problem isn't even aware of it and it is true that the most easily offended are people with little self-respect.

So look to your own self-respect and if you feel hurt about something that has happened between you and a friend or maybe between you and your wife or husband, think again and ask yourself is it worth damaging a good relationship just because your pride is hurt.

Bernard Baruch, the distinguished American diplomat and socialite, always said he let his dinner guests seat themselves. If they ended up in the wrong company he never worried. As he put it "The people who mind don't matter, and the people who matter don't mind".

Remember that saying the next time you feel hurt about something and decide whether you are going to choose to be someone who minds or someone who matters!

If you are in control of your life and your destiny you are the one who can afford to be generous. You can afford to step back in the shade and let the other person shine. Remember you are becoming a winner by helping others to success.

You can afford a personal modesty. Of course you can enjoy the fruits of your success. It's one of the reasons for pursuing it. But have a look at your motives. Are you secure in your success or do you need your £100,000 yacht permanently moored in the Mediterranean or the Caribbean to prove it. You can use your visible success to motivate those you are helping on their way. Motive matters - but so does motivation!

If you are on your way don't undervalue yourself. We can all marvel at great natural achievements. In Britain people travel miles to wonder at the beauties of Scottish Highlands, the Lake District, Snowdonia or the Giant's Causeway.

The Sermon on the Mount reminds us of the beauties of the lilies of the field - but it goes on to say that if God so clothed them would he not be even more concerned about men.

Confidence is built on the experience of success. It is by developing confidence that we learn our skills from riding a bicycle to cooking a perfect meal. And yet we spend so much time looking back to failures.

My mother was a remarkable woman and in her later years she restored and rebuilt old semi-derelict houses in many parts of Northern Ireland. She always used direct labour and was her own 'Clerk of Works'. She ordered the raw materials, calculated costs and managed each venture in detail - negotiating grants with planners as she went along. And yet in spite of these achievements, in spite of controlling her small investments and keeping an eye on her shares which she bought and sold at regular intervals, she always insisted that she "was no good at Maths".

This extraordinary determination to insist on that failure persisted all her days. Thank God that her positive determination and achievements far outweighed this little piece of negative thinking. For too many people time is spent and wasted on searching out and cultivating opportunities for such a negative attitude.

Self respect will show itself in many different ways. We have spoken of attitudes and relationships. It is important to realise that a simple thing such as personal appearance and good grooming can convey a message in itself. If you can walk into a room on a social occasion or into a business conference knowing that you are looking your best it will increase your confidence in that situation.

If you are trying to set standards for others, don't expect them to believe in them unless they can see that you are applying them to yourself.

As far as appearance is concerned, it is a matter of fact that we will usually be instantly judged by our looks which make the first and lasting impression. We can't do much about our physical features but we should make an effort to take care of health and appearance, to make the best of what we have. We behave as we think we look and those of us who can learn to be fairly satisfied with our physical features have given ourselves another part of the Winning Start.

Where you can, take control of yourself in any situation. Be in charge and know where you are going. But don't become so detached about yourself that you forget the value or the impact of emotion. If you are too impersonal about yourself coldness can take charge and freeze out communication.

My daughter's wedding was a wonderful happy occasion and I had planned and written my speech. As a family we had come through some tough times and I felt that here was an opportunity to say a public "Thank you" to them all. I must have underestimated emotion. Quite suddenly in the middle of my speech I almost ground to a halt. I did manage to keep going somehow and I said the things I wanted to say - but I very nearly allowed the planning and calculation to be blotted out by the impact of sudden and unexpected emotion. Be ready to feel for other people but never be afraid to feel for yourself.

Most people who have made a success of their lives have learnt that they each have unique qualities which they have developed. They are at ease with that knowledge and they are not afraid to have other people recognise those unique elements that make them different.

When we speak of equality we must realise that individuals have different abilities both physical and mental. At the same time everyone is entitled to the equality of a fair share of the fulfilment available to those who have been able to reach their own potential.

Try these exercises for self-respect.

1) Dress and look your best.

2) Make a list of the good reasons for respecting yourself.

3) Set your own standards for yourself. Don't accept them second hand.

4) Give your name first when you meet someone new. Look them in the eye.

5) Be ready to say "Thank you" when anyone pays you a compliment.

6) Make a plan for improvement in yourself. Refer to it and revise it regularly.

7) Smile.

I am lucky enough to be responsible for training our local Church choir. I encourage them to smile as they sing. As I have often said to them "People can hear the smile in your singing!". Try it - it's true.

Be someone you can respect

Tactics (3)

Create and Develop a Positive Image or Yourself

As we have talked about becoming a winner the stress has consistently been placed on attitude and making the commitment involved in taking the basic decision to follow the winner's path. That is absolutely right. Without decision and commitment there is no prospect of success.

However no-one sensible sets out on a journey or starts work on a task without having an idea of where they are going or what they hope to achieve. So when you come to the moment of decision ask yourself two questions

1) What kind of person am I?

2) What kind of person do I want to be?

Defeatists will tell you that human nature can't be changed, that man is essentially a self-centred and selfishly motivated creature. If that is the whole truth then we may as well pack up our bags and give up now. But of course it isn't true.

For all animals natural instincts are concerned with ensuring continuing existence and with the survival of the species.

Without those instincts they would soon cease to exist. As the ages have passed and environments have changed, some species have failed to meet these criteria and have become extinct. We all know what happened to the dinosaurs.

Through the centuries as man has evolved and developed there have been many examples of the fate of the dinosaur befalling men and nations which have not been ready to accept the need for change.

Great industries have collapsed. Great nations and great empires have faded from their former glories. But time and time again new life has sprung from the ashes of past achievements. Men and women with new ideas, new imagination and new approaches to life have emerged to lead in the new directions needed.

So when you ask yourself the second question "What kind of person do I want to be?", don't be afraid to dream. Don't let your imagination be hemmed in by the walls of past experience.

It's sometimes frightening to realise the extent to which our decisions and our determination can be negatively ruled by previous failure. Of course, if you want to, you can avoid a challenge by the simple decision to say to yourself "I've never been able to do that before". If that's your decision then be prepared to accept responsibility for spending the rest of your life in the loser's lane.

Anyone who is old enough to have been taught handwriting by the use of an old-fashioned copy book will remember the laborious business of writing out proverbs and sayings time after time. One of them may well have been

"If at first you don't succeed, try and try and try again".

It may be obvious and simple, but it certainly isn't a bad beginning. From now on the motto is going to be "That is my dream and nothing is going to stop me from fulfilling it". Above all else don't let anyone else steal your dream. Jealous friends or people who feel frightened by the challenge to themselves of what they see you doing will try their best to discourage you.

The day you decide to stop smoking it is important to refuse an offered cigarette with "No thanks, I don't smoke" and not with "No thanks, I've given them up". To someone else who still smokes the **non**-smoker is no problem whereas the **ex**-smoker represents a challenge to their own ability to control their addiction. Treat alcohol or any other bad habits the same way. "I don't" rather than "I've stopped" or "I've given it up". Apart from the effect your words may have on others, the constant repetition of your new position following your own decision strengthens your own commitment to it.

Human nature can be changed. And in particular for each of us our own nature can be changed. It is a matter of combining decision with attitude, and attitude is very important.

There were remarkable results in a primary school where a young teacher (who had let the parents know what she was doing) walked into class one day and told the children that she had just read about a remarkable discovery. Scientists had carried out experiments which showed that children with blue eyes were brighter and learnt better than those with brown eyes. Each child was asked to wear a sign marked 'blue eyes' or 'brown eyes'. Within a few weeks the level of achievement of the 'brown eyes' began to fall while that of the 'blue eyes' improved. Then one day the teacher came in and told the children that she had made a big mistake. She had got the story wrong. The scientists had really discovered that it was the brown-eyed children who were brighter and the light-coloured blue-eyed ones who were not so intelligent. Extraordinarily the performance levels of the two groups immediately began to swing back in the opposite directions.

Looking back to teenage days I can remember that there were always 'wallflowers' among the girls. The ones who were convinced that they weren't pretty enough for anyone to want to dance with them. Very often the way they stood or sat half-hidden in a corner helped to discourage boys from approaching them and underlined their own lack of belief in themselves.

In a business setting the same negative attitude can have disastrous effects on sales. Unless a salesman believes in his ability to sell, no matter how good the quality of the product, he will not achieve the performance of others who believe in their ability even though they may be offering a product of less proven quality.

Miles was a boy in the same class with me at school. He was always in trouble. He was big and strong and brash and a bit of a bully. He had been expelled from more than one primary school as unmanageable. As you can imagine he always sat in the back row of the class and caused as much disruption as he could. One morning he was summoned to the headmaster's study. We all assumed the worst. But what had actually happened?

Without a word to anyone Miles had written an essay about missionary work in India and had entered it in a national competition. What inspired him he never told us. But he won the national prize. He became a reformed character. He joined the school choir, he suddenly moved to the front row in class, he became a school prefect. His whole concept of himself changed and he went on to have a most successful career in later life.

Many people suffer from attitude problems - wallflowers, tearaways, unsuccessful salesmen, ineffective priests, poor teachers - they can be found in all walks of life.

People who are determined to be winners will not only change their own attitude but they will soon discover that they can help others by a simple awareness of their problems. If you can convince someone that you genuinely like them they suddenly begin to realise that if someone else likes them, why shouldn't they begin to like themselves.

When we talked of respect for ourselves in an earlier section I said that it was important to accept our physical selves as the basic equipment with which we had to work. It is up to us to make the best use of what we are born with.

There are hundreds of thousands of great achievers among people who suffer from the severest handicap, physical or mental. Watch the determination and dedication of participants in Paralympic competitions or read a book like Professor Stephen Hawking's A Brief History of Time and you will realise that no handicap can be allowed to be put forward as an excuse for not making the effort to be a winner.

Traditionally our society admires the 'modest hero'. Even those with great achievements are encouraged to play them down. "It must have been luck". "Anyone would have done the same". But too much modesty, too much writing down of our efforts can have a cumulative negative impact.

Even though it wouldn't be a good idea to go round telling other people what a wonderful person you are, you should practise talking positively to yourself. What good things can you tell yourself? Make a list!

"I can cook"
"I get on with other people"
"I have a sense of humour"
"I'm a good dancer"
"I get good results at work"
"I keep my word"
"I'm reliable"
"I love my wife/husband"

Make a good enough job of your list and at the end of it you might be able to add "I know where I'm going" and "I like myself".

For example, when I tell my wife that I know I'm just marvellous, she laughs! But then I believe that's because she loves me and she knows the truth of the matter.

While I have been writing this book my wife and I have discussed many aspects of what I have been planning to say. One of these areas is the whole question of feminine achievement. Looking round the world there are clear signs in all walks of life that women are setting their sights on the top. There are very few activities where they cannot be found among the highest achievers. I am pleased and delighted that this is so and that women are setting targets for themselves as winners in politics, in business, in the professions or wherever else their ambitions lie. It is right that everyone should have the same opportunity of achievement whatever their background, or sex or colour or other classification that might seek to divide them.

I have raised the point of feminine achievement for one special reason. I stop agreeing with those who argue for equal opportunity (which should not be denied) when they go so far out along the road of their own conviction that they undervalue the way of life of those who have decided that their 'winning' pattern of life lies in more traditional fields.

There are literally millions of women who have dedicated their lives to the family where they play the central role of wife and mother. John Paul Getty said that to be successful you must build your success on the successes of others. When a woman can look around her and see a husband with whom she shares a deep and loving relationship and a family in which the children are happy and living constructive cared-for lives, she has every right to say to herself "I am a winner!"

Once the family has grown up and left to fend for themselves there will of course be new opportunities to develop skills, to explore new fields of adventure, to take on new responsibilities. Very often these can be interwoven with the life of home-building. As long as a woman can say to herself "I am doing what I ought to be doing and I am doing it to the best of my ability", no-one, whatever their own personal convictions about the role of women in society, has any right to downgrade or take away from the value of that woman's achievement.

When each of us creates and develops the positive image of ourselves as a winner, part of the plan will be setting goals for ourselves. Goals must balance ambition with a sense of reality. There would be no point in me setting myself the goal of winning the Olympic 100 metres title. Linford Christie could give me at least 50 metres start and still win comfortably. On the other hand at the moment I am writing this book against a time table which I have set myself because the pre-determined decision to have the first draft completed by a fixed date gives me a basic discipline that will help achieve the ultimate goal.

Disciplining yourself by setting short term goals or targets is an excellent means of making sure that long term goals are reached. When you decide that being a winner is for you, one of the first challenges you will face is to establish a series of meaningful goals long-term, intermediate and short-term. It is a good idea to have a mixture of major ambitions and lesser challenges. If your goal is to climb to the top of the mountain on the far horizon you will be able to do it by travelling to the nearest stand of trees and then moving on from there.

Set yourself a straightforward but personally challenging first target - one that may be quickly done but will need guts to do it.

Go and apologise to someone for something you have said or done that affects them. It may take a bit of nerve to summon up the courage to do it, but once it has been done you may well find that by that simple action you have already begun to create a new relationship.

Whatever your short term plans may be, keep the long term goals in your mind. Remind yourself of them at least once every day during the thirty minutes you set aside for quiet reflection on where you are going and how you are planning to get there. By keeping them fresh you may well find that some of the small things you have achieved have left you with a new perspective. The target may be the same, but the angle of approach may have changed.

When that happens it will be up to you to make the necessary adjustments to your own target mechanisms. It is important to know and understand the target. As you keep it in mind you can see yourself achieving it. That in turn develops a positive mental attitude to the plan and positive attitude is an essential element of success.

Imagination - or the creation of images in the mind - of what each of us can be is a positive force. By seeing ourselves achieving our goals we create a new power controlling our personal development.

Anyone involved in physical activity knows of the importance of training. Without training, ambition is pointless. Equally it is true that mental rehearsal of success (or imagination and its power) can enhance performance. When you get an opportunity to watch great high jumpers in competition, particularly in close-up on television, it is fascinating to watch them rehearse the run-up in their minds. As they get ready to move they plant each imaginary footstep on the way and even begin to hoist themselves off the ground in the imagination. They rehearse success so that they approach the bar with confidence.

There is another fascination which tells us much of human nature and how it tries to reclaim control of our lives. I have watched a jumper clear a bar by several inches. The commentator tells us what the athlete already knows. That was a personal best. Up goes the bar to the next height - another 2 centimetres, less than an inch. What happens? The bar gets knocked down - often because it is approached with no conviction. The built-in expectation of failure can be a terrible handicap.

I play golf usually scoring in the low to middle 80's. One day I struck a purple streak in a match. I posted five consecutive birdies! Nothing too startling for an expert but unheard of in my experience. I arrived on the ninth tee standing 2 under par. For the first time in my life I had the prospect of breaking par over a nine hole stretch. Suddenly I was convinced that I couldn't do it. Although I did manage to avoid driving out of bounds into the sea on my left, I somehow managed to drop three shots on the one hole. Shame - wasn't it! And yet just another example of the uncomfortable power of negative thinking.

But what excitement when the opposite happens. I remember watching Mary Peters in the Pentathlon High Jump at the Munich Olympics. Mary was on her way to a Gold Medal. Suddenly she produced three consecutive personal best High Jumps in succession. She was flying! That day everything was in place. Thinking, performing, imagination and action all came together. She was a winner.

It is important, at the same time, that we don't kid ourselves and then end up blaming the system.

No-one will achieve success by setting what they know are unrealistic targets. Your goals must be related to your true potential. There are plenty of helpful hints to encourage positive thinking. Cutting out pictures of dream cars, dream houses, dream holiday locations and sticking them on the shaving mirror or the door of the fridge. Reading books like this one. Listening to tapes of winners speaking. There is no doubt that all these things help, but without a realistic inner decision and a personal dedication and input they will ultimately lead nowhere.

For far too many years most of us have fed ourselves on the drip-feed diet of defeatism. The step across the line of decision and the determination to throw out the old me and start on the new one, with all the commitment that will demand, is the vital move. If you are not prepared to start climbing the ladder - even to begin with if it only means putting your foot on the first rung - it doesn't really matter where it reaches. You won't be getting there.

You may find that this is offering you the temptation to go for the easy option and to settle for the second-best. Don't fall for it. Short term goals that you can achieve are well worthwhile. They can give you a sense of achievement. But they must be a part of a more imaginative overall plan for a long term goal.

Gary Player heard a spectator shout out "Lucky" when he holed a bunker shot. Player's answer stated a simple truth "It's a remarkable thing, but I've noticed that the more I practise, the luckier I get".

Practice for success is an essential part of winning. In the early stages there will be a pattern of trial and error. After a while the pattern will change to trial and success and as long as practice is maintained the pattern will eventually become continuous success without the need for trial.

Sometimes winning at one level is not enough. Nick Faldo was a winner at the top of the European Money Winners but he wasn't satisfied. He knew he could be better. His goal was to be the best. So he dismantled his whole golf game and built it up again to a new pattern.

As a result of that decision he now holds the record for the longest tenure of World Ranking Number One. This is real winning - setting yourself the goal of your highest potential and fighting through until you achieve it.

Useful practice exercises for improving your image of yourself

1) At least once a month set out to find out all you can about someone you know to be a winner.

2) Sit down and write out a two-page list of all your positive assets. Don't be limited by past experience - make the effort to draw on your potential - look at it as an exercise in applying for the job of the rest of your own life.

3) Take the time to have a look at the physical picture you present to the world. Think about what you can do to improve it. Clear out the clutter that surrounds and conceals the real you.

4) Cut down on your TV watching and use the time to do something constructive. Get the family to do the same. Rediscover the joy of living and playing together.

5) When things go right for you tell yourself "That's the real me". When they go wrong - which they surely sometimes will - tell yourself, "Come on, I can do better than that".

6) Constantly remind yourself of the goals you have achieved as you think of the goals still ahead - Remember, success is contagious.

Create and develop a positive image for yourself

Tactics (4)

Great Expectations

The whole process of becoming a winner is made up of different aspects - all of them important. First there is the determination to be honest - particularly with yourself. Then there is the realisation that you must make yourself into the kind of person that you yourself would want to like and respect. The third step is to build pictures of yourself as you feel you can and ought to be - what is often called 'goal-setting'. I have already mentioned this part of the process and I have tried to distinguish between the long-term dream which can be as ambitious as you care to make it and the short-term steps along the way towards that dream, the short-term goals which you are likely to be able to reach.

The measure of the likelihood of your reaching even those short-term goals can be easily described as your own self-expectancy or what you honestly expect that you can achieve.

Your expectations for yourself can be negative or positive. When they are negative it is amazing how often the thing which you fear may go wrong is the very thing that happens. When you are invited to a party or any social function by someone you don't know very well what is your reaction? Do you say to yourself

"I'm not going to enjoy it. I won't know anyone" - because if you do, unless you meet some very positive thinkers among the other guests, that's exactly what will happen and you will come home depressed, saying to your companion "I knew it was going to be like that".

On the other hand when you receive the invitation, do you say "I'd love to go! This will be a real opportunity to make new friends and a change from our usual activities". If that is your reaction you will have an interesting evening, meeting new and apparently cheerful and positive people with every chance that you will benefit from a widening social circle.

These ideas can be summarised quite simply:

If your expectations are negative, what you fear most is likely to happen.

If your expectations are positive, what you expect and hope for is likely to happen.

The level of your achievement, and we hope it will be upwards, will be the consequence of your genuine expectations for yourself. So remember - Unless you **consciously plan differently** your inbuilt expectancy will take control.

Unfortunately much of our early training tends to produce negative thinking and attitudes, so if you want to change the direction of your expectations for your own future you have to train your thinking into new paths. You have indeed consciously to plan differently, consciously to take your expectations firmly in both hands and point them in a positive direction.

As you stand looking at the hill in front of you, don't think to yourself "I doubt if I will make it to the top". With that expectation you will stop half-way up, exhausted in spirit and in hope. No, when you look at the hill and think about climbing it, say to yourself "That's not going to be too hard for me - and I just know that the view from the top is going to be fantastic". With those thoughts in your mind nothing will stop you and you will probably bring several others to the top of the hill with you.

When you think about goals for yourself remember that the highest image or goal that you set will be pointless and have no inspiration for you if you don't expect in your own mind that you are going to reach it. In parallel with that realisation it is good to know that winners who set goals for themselves and genuinely expect to reach them are already probably half-way there.

To get yourself into a positive frame of mind for your goal-setting plans establish good practice for yourself. Set short-term goals that you can achieve. Don't duck the challenge of setting your long-term targets high - to do that would be to get into the habit of accepting the soft option. Have your ultimate dream as the shining light and the guiding star, but don't miss the opportunity of getting early into the positive habit of goal attainment.

Look at this simple example from the world of sales.

Our salesman goal-setter has just completed a year in which he sold 1000 units - an average of 20 units a week. If he says to himself "I'm going to sell twice as many units next year" he will immediately have a target of selling 40 units a week - which could be enough to put him off - even from trying.

But suppose he says to himself "I'm going to sell one more unit this week than last week" and keeps the same target throughout the year - just simply increasing his sales figure by one unit from week to week. That sounds fairly straightforward and certainly not too frightening. Now sit down with a piece of paper and do a little mathematics. If he sells for 50 weeks and works to that pattern he will sell over 2300 units in the year. Long-term goal more than achieved!

Perhaps you don't think that those figures are realistic. Maybe they aren't. But think further about them and look at your own level of performance in whatever you do. Suppose an increase of one unit a week is too much for you. Think about one unit a month and work out the effect for yourself.

Do you subscribe to your church? Do you give £1 a week? What would happen if you gave an extra 10p a week this month? Would you miss it? I doubt it. Then another extra 10p a week next month. Again you wouldn't miss it. Do you realise that by this time next year you would be giving £2.20 each week - or more than double! I would hate to alarm you, but suppose you are already able to be more generous in your giving and start from £5 a week. Try putting that up by 50p per week for one month and then doing the same again each month for a year. I guarantee that if every subscriber to your church did the same, any financial problems the church may be having would be a thing of the past in no time.

Wherever you stand or whatever you are thinking about, motivation is not something optional. There is no such thing as 'neutral' when you consider motivation. It exists whether you make a decision or not. You should realise that where you have made no decision "because that doesn't matter to me" then your motivation is already negative because not only will you be doing nothing yourself, but your attitude will be rubbing off on others.

Thankfully motivation can be learned and developed. It is not an inborn quality. You can focus your own attention on any subject and ask yourself "Where do I stand?" and "What am I doing (or going to do) about it?" You can talk to others and discuss attitudes with them.

Particularly if they are winners themselves and have positive attitudes the likelihood is that they will challenge you to **raise the standard of your own motivation.**

Notice those words **raise the standard of your own motivation.** They are very significant. Throughout the world of business and personal options you will come across people who are trying to increase your motivation - through incentives, pep talks, rallies, self-help books like this one (!), through sermons or through challenges. Certainly all these things can help. But they can only help the individual to develop their own motivation and turn on their own capacity for further achievement **if they want to!** The decision has to come from within.

Once the decision has been taken and the switch has been turned to the 'ON' position, no matter if things go wrong from time to time - which they surely will - the positive motivational determination will be there to bring you back on track. With this question of motivation, which is so clearly self-motivation, remember too the value of sharing your determination with other positive thinkers who are also on the way to being winners.

In very general terms there are two major motivational aspects - fear and desire.

Fear is negative. It draws pictures of failure, of the obligations of success, of previous bad experience.
It creates negative tension within you.

Negative or destructive tension can be directly responsible for personal distress, for anxiety, for sickness; it can introduce personal hostility and that in turn can lead to rejection and the destruction of personal relationships.

The only time when fear could be seen to produce positive results is when you are motivated by fear of the consequences of failure.

The language of fear is littered with phrases like "I can't", "I don't think I could", "I don't want to" or "I suppose I have to". All of these are designed to anticipate probable failure and all indicate a frame of mind that is likely to produce failure as an end product.

The opposite motivator 'Desire' is positive. And it is important to separate it as a concept from human selfishness.

Desire is the sense of positive determination. It attracts. It reaches out to others. It encourages. It achieves.

Desire draws on positive past experience, memory of pleasure and success.

Desire and determination can introduce positive tension and stress.

Where negative tension will stretch you to breaking point, positive tension will tune your strings to the true pitch where they sound the right notes and on which you can play the song of success. Positive tension brings expectation and anticipation of good things. The language of Desire and Determination is decorated with phrases like "I can", "I will", "I am going to", "I want to" (N.B. not **"I want"**).

So the two motivators have their own languages, their own attitudes and their own tensions. Is the tension good or bad? That depends on the direction in which you are aiming. Don't be afraid of feeling the tension of decision making. If you feel no tension you are either comatose or dead!

Expectation then rises from internal thought, internal motivation, internal decision. Remember the saying "As a man thinketh in his heart, so he becomes". This promise is true for everyone - for young or old, for man or woman, for black or white, for East or West. It explains why those responsible for ideological training have always put so much effort into early education and the development of thought.

If you can pre-condition the thinking process you have won more than half the battle for the mind. That is why it is so vitally important for each of us, you and me, to become aware of how we think, to be determined to free ourselves from bad pre-conceptions and to take responsibility for the direction of our own thoughts from here on in.

"As a man thinketh in his heart, so he becomes". The way we think decides the way we act so if we want to move our lives in a positive direction we must direct our thinking along positive paths.

The man who is presented with a problem and immediately starts thinking about a solution is much more likely to solve it than the man who tries to identity the difficulties. The winner says "When I have £100 I will be able to do this" and sets out to put together £100. The loser looks at the same situation and says "What a pity I haven't got £100. I'm afraid I can't even begin".

[This next paragraph is self-defeating because by writing it down I am doing exactly what I am advising you not to do! When you are offering motivation to someone whatever you do don't use phrases that begin with the words "Whatever you do don't do so and so!". Perhaps the person listening to your advice had never even thought of doing it in the first place.]

Anyhow now that you have read the paragraph you can draw a pencil line through it and leave it out the next time you read this chapter. By then you won't need to be reminded! In fact now that I have finished writing it out, I am going to get the printer to draw the line through it for you.

As a matter of habit, winners have well-targeted goals in their minds and they keep them well to the front. They **expect** positive results and that expectation leads to fulfilment. On the other hand, losers dwell on the negatives; they live in the expectation of failure or disaster. If they go out for an evening it never surprises them if they receive bad service or poor food or just generally have a dull time. Redundancy when it comes has an unerring habit of picking them out. In a recession, as a result of their negative expectations, they are among the first whose companies collapse into bankruptcy. Even when it comes to such an apparently unconnected thing as their health, if there's an epidemic about they will expect to catch it; they expect to feel bad and they do.

Scientists and medical experts are increasingly beginning to accept that attitude and expectation can affect health even in such apparently unlikely areas as being liable to physical accident or pregnancy. 'Psychosomatic illness' are not just a pair of long words. The mind (the Psyche) can control and effect the body (the Soma). Stressful changes in life or anxious expectations tie in with the body's immune system.

On the positive side we know that the body produces defence mechanisms to deal with emergencies. We have all experienced the mind-sharpening rush of adrenaline.

Goose pimples designed to make the hair stand erect and improve the body's insulation in cold weather. At the same time we often hear of people being described as run down and depressed - a condition that can arise from continuous negative thinking which can reduce the body's natural ability to fight and resist infection.

Negative tensions can be induced in other people. Modern research into asthma in children has shown that it can be made worse by the loving protectiveness of caring parents whose anxiety transmits itself to the child, which in turn makes the asthma attacks worse. Although it may appear cruel and rather heartless, at least one hospital specialising in this childhood complaint has introduced 'parentectomy' - cutting off the parents from the child - as an effective preliminary step in dealing with the symptoms of children's asthma.

Another classic area in which there has been evidence of the impact of mind over body is in those tribal societies in Africa and Australia where witch doctors or medicine men have long been known to have the power of what we might call 'thinking people to death'. Most usually the impact of their actions can be seen as soon as the target victim becomes aware of the existence of the spell which has been cast. Similar traditions exist in parts of the West Indies and some of the Southern United States where the traditions of the Voodoo culture still hold sway.

To an extraordinary degree attitude and self-expectancy can have similar impacts in other fields. The person who fears that things will go wrong and who goes into a situation expecting failure comes out with nothing.

The winner on the other hand has learnt about the effectiveness of self-fulfilling prophecy. He has kept up an upward momentum in life by expecting a better job, good health, financial gain, warm friendships and success. When the winner faces a problem he sees it as a challenge to his ability and determination to overcome it. The loser looks at it, sighs defeatedly, maybe makes an ineffective effort to solve it and turns away.

One of the most astonishing examples of a winner's attitude changing the whole shape of an event was in the England/Australia Test Match at Headingley in 1981. Australia batted first and declared at 401 for 9. In their first innings England made a miserable 174 and were forced to follow on. Even in their second innings things began badly and they were 105 for 5 wickets when Ian Botham came in. At lunch time on the second last day the bookies on the ground were offering odds of 1000 - 1 against England (odds so attractive that they even tempted two of the Australian side to bet £5 on England!).

Suddenly in mid-afternoon when two more wickets had fallen and England drooped sadly at 135 for 7, Botham, aided by fast bowler Graham Dilley, took command. With enormous confidence they began to smash the ball all over the ground. Defeat which had seemed certain that day was delayed and the team's cancelled hotel bookings had to be re-instated. With the help of Dilley and the other two bowlers, Old and Willis, Botham roared on to reach a personal score of 149 not out and the innings eventually closed at 356 just 130 runs ahead.

In the final innings Australia were cruising to victory at 56 for one wicket when the fire that had burned in Botham's belly lit a response in Bob Willis. Wickets began to crash and amid extraordinary scenes Willis took 8 for 43 as England scraped home by 18 runs.

The winner's attitude personified in Ian Botham, as so often happens, had rubbed off on others - particularly on Bob Willis who was equally inspired. I often ask myself what the sub-conscious effects of those £5 bets may have been on the Australian camp. I'm sure they all thought it was a great joke at the time when the bets were made - but if you put money on the opposition you must be planting even the smallest seed of doubt somewhere. We can only wonder when the first realisation of the possibility of defeat began to assume reality in Australian minds.

Over the last years there has been a steady and depressing change in the attitude of the media to sports performance. Particularly in England there has been a development of a negative expectation as the underlying theme and the effect of this approach can be seen in the negative attitude of managers and players.

Look at the English football team. For years they never expected to lose. Then skills spread and developed elsewhere. Looking at today's results it is hard to realise that it was not until 1953 that

England lost any international match at the national stadium to any team from outside the United Kingdom.

Nowadays the fear of failure in most cases outweighs the positive plan to win. Every time international commitments arise, journalists swarm around demanding winning performances and trumpeting 'Crucial Tie'. They induce negative thinking in the minds of management and those selected and then they bay for blood when the team achieves negative results.

With very few exceptions Managers have stopped thinking like winners. They go into games looking for 'a result'. The word 'win' has disappeared from the vocabulary. Playing away from home they think defensively.

At the time of the Rugby World Cup in 1991 the English Rugby Team was the strongest for years. A mighty pack and brilliant attacking backs were taught and trained to play a tight game. The philosophy was clear to see. "If the other side don't score, we can't lose". When the team reached the World Cup Final they knew that they had to win - Not losing was no longer enough. So they decided to play to their brilliant skills. Unfortunately disuse had dulled the shining edge and although they made a gallant effort it wasn't enough. Who knows what might have happened if there had been a different approach right along the line.

Of course in any winner's strategy there must be a place for defence, but it should never be allowed to snuff out the stuff of adventure and the polishing of winning skills. If you send your players onto the field full of the idea "We must not lose", how much mental capacity is left for the conviction "We are going to win"?

It is seldom by accident that a nation suddenly emerges as a winning force on the international sporting scene. The change can almost always be traced to the impact of a single person - either a performer or a coach. Example breeds success. "If he can, I can!" or from the coach "You can be better and I can show you how".

When I was at school in Dublin there was a simple example. My own event was the half-mile (now the 800 metres!). I found myself running in the Inter Schools final and half way round the second lap I realised that I could win. I became a winner almost by accident. The clock showed afterwards that even my modest time had improved my best by 4 seconds. The limits of my potential had been unexpectedly stretched. From that day onwards I expected to win against other schools and I was disappointed when I didn't.

A new coach arrived and standards changed. Others knew that if I could do it so could they and our small school with only 150 boys produced 4 Irish champions from the same material. The coach's attitude was 'Be prepared to try new techniques and expect to be able to do better'. Results proved him right. Our athletic attitude changed from "I don't expect" into "I don't see why I shouldn't be able to". The results spoke for themselves.

Don't expect miracles unless you are prepared to support your expectation with honest effort. When the man prayed for a miracle that he would win a prize from the National Lottery he had no cause for complaint when, as he prayed for the third time, an impatient voice spoke from heaven to say "Will you at least go out and buy a ticket!" - not that the National Lottery should be anyone's idea of a highway to success!

Develop the techniques of optimism. If you don't expect success you are very unlikely to achieve it. The salesman who makes no conscious effort to sell isn't going to top the list of achievers.

When I knew that I was going to Africa in 1970, I had to take a British car since I was on a Government-funded scheme. I wanted a Sunbeam Alpine and the main Belfast sales room was just across the street from where I worked. I went in to buy. Two salesmen stood talking to each other and paid no attention as I walked round the car I had selected. No notice was taken so I left.

I went next door to the salesroom of the Triumph distributor. As I walked in, I was cheerfully greeted "Can I help you?". I explained my situation. The salesman was interested and enthusiastic. Within 30 minutes I left having ordered a new Triumph 2000 specially adapted for African road conditions to be delivered to me in Malawi. I had never even driven one when I signed the deal. I loved the car. The salesmen in the first establishment may well not have expected me to buy. The Triumph salesman certainly expected to sell!

Thinking of Africa reminds me of the situation I found there. Many people have criticised the actions of Dr Banda who has been Prime Minister and later President of Malawi since independence in 1964. By our western standards the country was far from being a perfect democracy. Single party rule was the way of political life. Opposition was crushed with leaders sometimes locked up, sometimes driven into exile. But in the midst of this there stood this small man with a clear goal for his nation, a clear understanding of what he stood for and an iron will to succeed.

Dr Banda's view was that the first priority for the country was to become capable of standing on its own economic feet. He was prepared to accept help - even from South Africa - although I was there when he told the South African State President that he disagreed with what he represented. He defined an identity for the nation. He planned a programme of Malawianisation. Wherever possible he appointed Malawians to responsible positions to replace Europeans left behind from Colonial days.

Having been an active member and an Elder of the Presbyterian Church in Scotland where he had practised medicine, he had strict ideas on standards of personal morality and he insisted on their application as standards for the nation.

1964 was Malawi's first year of Independence. That year the national budget was £12 million of which £8 million came from the United Kingdom in grants and the remaining £4 million was raised by internal taxation. When I was in the country just eight years later I listened to the Minister's Budget Speech in which he projected an annual expenditure of £21 million and projected internal revenue at £22 million.

At today's values such figures are tiny but this was a poor country and in those eight years the change in achievement had been spectacular. Since then spells of poor rainfall and bad harvests have caused serious economic problems, but in spite of all that, tiny Malawi with perhaps 6,000,000 inhabitants has been able to take in more than 1 million refugees fleeing from civil war in neighbouring Mozambique.

When independence came to the countries of Central Africa, the one with the least physical and economic potential was undoubtedly Malawi.

However, one man's dream, one man's goal-setting and one man's determination (or expectancy) saw to the achievement of the near impossible. At the time of writing, the country is going through the difficult process of reforming political systems to allow for the next generation. Dr Banda who must be over 90 years old (the exact figure is never revealed) will have to step down from the Life Presidency which he took on in 1970. It will be interesting to see how his successors will manage and what kind of goals they will set and achieve over the country's next thirty years.

* * * * *

When it comes to planning to be a winner, this book has been offering a programme which can lead to success. First to be honest particularly with and about yourself. Second to value yourself as the kind of person you yourself would want to like. Thirdly to create a new image of what you have the potential to be. Now fourthly we have been looking at the impact on your achievement of expecting it to be the best.

Winners see risk as opportunity. They do not fear the penalties of failure because they do not see themselves in a failing situation. When Gary Player made his comment about "The more I practise - the luckier I seem to become" he was quite simply underlining a fact that all winners understand - the fact that so-called luck is most often the coming together of preparation and opportunity.

Opportunities abound in plenty but only those on the look out for them are in a position to make effective use of them. Winners only **seem** to be lucky because their positive expectations of life mean they are better prepared when opportunity offers.

The same attitudes of positive expectation are effective in the home and family. The enthusiasm of optimistic parents is contagious. Their good humour and ability to look on the bright side, to accentuate the positive, can be seen reflected in the attitudes and often in the achievements of the younger generation. Not only within the family, but in wider relationships, people are attracted by positive, self-assured and optimistic winners. Not so surprising is the fact that they are put off by pessimistic people with negative attitudes.

There is a growing body of medical evidence that when triggered by optimism the body produces substances called endorphins which can reduce pain and introduce a 'feel-good' factor. Artificial stimuli such as opium, alcohol, cocaine, morphine, LSD and marijuana have been used over the passage of time to try to induce optimism or a feeling of well-being. Unfortunately they too often end up with a let-down or hangover reaction and have the constant problem of potential addiction.

Endorphins either reduce pain or increase the body's capacity to accept higher levels of it. Women in labour are known to secrete endorphins which help them to get through the pain of giving birth to the desirable end. If, as is suspected, optimism in general can encourage the production of endorphins it would seem to be the intelligent thing to do to train your thinking along optimistic lines.

Avoid getting tied in to pessimists. Negative thinkers love to have someone to share their misery. So if you find yourself talking to a pessimist take a deliberate positive line with them. Stress the fact that you are concentrating your efforts on making the world a better place to be in - for yourself, for your friends and all those whom you meet.

If the pessimist asks how you come to be so cheerful you can always tell them that you are 'high' on a new drug called 'endorphine'. When they ask how to get hold of it, tell them about it and advise them to try and induce a dose for themselves by switching attitude to a more optimistic view of life.

Regular Exercises to Improve Expectation

1) Wake up happy - You **can** learn how. Wake up to music and start the day by showing a positive face to people as you meet them.

2) Talk positively to yourself. "Today is a good day for me". "This is my best year so far".

3) See every problem as an opportunity for achievement.

4) Concentrate all your energy on whatever is your most important project. Remember when you complete it, your achievement will give you a shot in the arm.

5) Look for good elements in all your personal relationships and concentrate on building them up.

6) Stay relaxed and friendly with other people even when you feel personal tension or stress.

7) Be positive about your own health and don't fuss too much about minor ailments.

8) Expect the best from others and encourage them to aim for it.

9) Associate with optimists.

Have Great Expectations

Tactics (5)

Time to decide

If you have been taking the opportunity to put the ideas you have been reading in this book into practice, by now you will have been trying to be honest with yourself. You will have been thinking about what you may have to do to gain your own respect and to deserve the respect of others. You will have set yourself down to think out what you ought to be able to become and you will have given some thought to how you can realistically expect to achieve the most from your potential. All these thoughts and actions are valid parts of the process of becoming a winner.

But when it comes to the question of who is going to become that winner - who is going to activate the opportunity to gain a Winning Start for the rest of their lives, then we have come to the moment of decision. Whatever else they may or may not be, winners are decision makers. They have thought their lives through using the kind of pattern outlined in these pages or something very similar. They have put together a package for themselves and their future and they have said "That is for me; that is what I am going for and I am prepared to make whatever personal commitment that package and that programme may call for".

Remembering always to steer away from purely selfish attitudes, success can be defined as a continuous process of realising goals that are worthy of you. Goals that stretch your potential and give you a real sense of achievement when they are accomplished.

These goals will not be easy options, they will not be self-centred options but they will follow guiding stars into paths of action that involve others and which will bring benefits to them as well as to yourself. When you make the momentous decision for action you must do so realising the need to have a purpose.

We all know that it is possible to enjoy some sort of life lazily, an unchallenging life with no risk, a life where you accept the comfortable option of leaving your destiny in other people's hands so long as they pay you adequately and don't expect too much effort or commitment in return. But you know in your heart that if you accept that pattern you are selling your true self short. Where is the satisfaction?

There's really one simple question. If you are travelling along the road of life without knowing where you are going, what chance have you of getting anywhere?

Studies of the survivors of the horrors of the concentration camps and death camps of World War II have shown quite clearly that while most of those who died had no choice or control over their fate and no opportunity to affect their future, a high proportion of those who did come through the awfulness had a clear purpose in mind - a personal motivation behind their determination to survive. Invariably they were people who whatever the odds resolutely refused to give up hope.

If you ever meet someone who is totally negative or who has given up all hope, try to remind him that for everyone - no matter how depressing their circumstances - life is expecting something of him. Life asks a contribution of everyone and it is up to each person to discover what that contribution should be. This is not a heartless or impersonal challenge. From the dying man the contribution may be as little as a smile, an acknowledgment of love or a brief prayer of thanks for past things achieved.

Look at the world today, particularly the world of the western democracies. It is full of people searching for an identity, for an answer to life, for a sense of belonging. In their desperation they try anything, the latest fashion fad, drugs, the mind-numbing negativism of punk or heavy metal raves, the weird world of cults from the Moonies to the Davidians. Anywhere where they will find someone to take over responsibility for their lives.

The first time I heard the saying it came from an old friend of my father's. He put it like this:

If you don't stand for something you'll fall for anything .

And make no mistake, the world is full of people just waiting to fall - often with tragic results for themselves or for their families from whom they are separated.

Today we live in a world of manipulators. Advertisers and PR men know it. Writers, playwrights, film makers, journalists, commentators and other media personalities line up behind an aggressive conventional **immorality, yes immorality.** They create a world in which immoral behaviour and attitudes seem the norm and by doing so they are able to avoid challenging their own life-styles, their own failure to set decent standards for their own lives.

People in the media constantly demand freedom for themselves and for their actions and decisions. In the service of some kind of liberalism they demand the right to act as they see fit and they reject the right of others to criticise the way they use the freedom they have grabbed. They will attack other people in the public eye from politicians to pop singers, from princes to priests for lack of achievement, for lack of responsibility, for moral failure, often quite simply for not doing what the critic thinks they should.

Many of the criticisms may be justified but few critics are willing to accept the logical corollary that others should have the right to demand the same standards of them that they demand of others. Specifically they demand freedom but reject responsibility.

In my days in broadcasting management I had many arguments with journalists who were convinced that their only duty was to 'tell the truth'. The sad thing was that they would never allow that anyone who was not qualified as a journalist could have the right or the knowledge to make any assessment of what they judged to be the truth. Anyone who has lived or worked in any of the world's notorious trouble spots knows full well that all too often one man's truth is another man's lie.

From my own knowledge and experience of Northern Ireland, in any confrontation there will be as many versions of 'what really happened' as there are conflicting interests taking part in the situation. It may seem contradictory but even with pictures to back up words there are often times when truth is not truth and when what appear to be obvious facts are not facts at all.

A man or woman may surely demand freedom to act as they see fit but the price of that freedom is clear. They must be prepared to accept responsibility for the consequences of the exercise of the freedom they have demanded.

There is little doubt that the standards of 'acceptable morality' have changed over the past thirty years and equally clearly the most significant influence in bringing about that change has been television. Apologists will claim that they are only 'telling it as it is'.

It may be true that the standards demanded by Lord Reith in the early days of the BBC were too narrowly drawn but they were undoubtedly Christian standards set for a Christian country. For years those standards were maintained and supported by Reith's successors but in the early 1960's new influences took control of the BBC and those who exerted the influence were determined to destroy what they inherited. Even concepts like the 9.00 pm watershed for explicit material were constantly challenged.

Today, when rampant materialism holds sway, none of us should be afraid to stand up and say "It is time for a change - let us have our decency back". This is not a call for some ferocious puritanical censorship which will curtail the imaginative use of creative facilities. It is rather a challenge to those fortunate enough to be blessed with creative ability to use it to enrich rather than impoverish the lives of those who consume their output.

The Head of Drama in BBC TV in the mid-1960's wrote a memo to everyone in his department which read

"I am becoming increasingly disturbed by the number of bedroom scenes appearing in the drama department's output. There are many other ways of letting the viewer know that a man and a woman find each other sexually attractive. A good director will know what they are!".

A study of films made in current settings during the 1930's, 40's and 50's will show that a very high percentage of the characters smoked cigarettes. On average someone on screen lit a cigarette about every 2 or 3 minutes throughout the action. In those days a high percentage of adults smoked regularly and it is well documented that each time a cigarette was lit on screen you could see a parallel series of flickering lighters and matches as the action triggered imitation among the cinema audience. The manipulators from the tobacco industry never missed a trick.

Faced with all the pressures of the media and their standards of carping negativism it is essential that you are well prepared to counteract them in your own interest. So think about the purpose of your life as you make the important decision for your future.

As long as you are in charge of your life there is hope for the future. As long as there is hope there is room for dreams and when the dreams are set down and targeted they become goals. Goals can be analysed and plans made for their achievement. What are your goals as you read these words?

For many people their only purpose seems to be to get to the end of today so that they can do something similar tomorrow. They wander aimlessly through their own lives with no sense of direction, no challenge, no achievement and probably only occasional passing happiness. When there is 'nothing on the telly' they have no alternative plan. Perhaps in the long term they would say that their aim is to retire. Be warned - true retirement is lying flat on your back in a box with a lily in your hand!

It's strange but true that the life expectancy of those who retire completely is short. So even if you find yourself approaching some apparently magic figure like 60 or 65 or even 70 don't start to say "From that day on I don't need to plan or take any more responsibility - after all I've done my share". If you do, you may be depressed to find that to put it bluntly you've **had** your share as well and the light switches off. So whatever you do, don't give up on the goal-setting.

Here's a simple suggestion. Let one of your goals be this.

I am going to be the oldest person I know who sits down regularly and plans for the year ahead.

Perhaps you may not make it, but there's a fair chance that you will achieve a number of intermediate goals along the way!

It is worth realising that an unsatisfactory life takes up just as much energy as a planned one, probably more. If you never take decisions for your future you are never going to be free to develop along the roads you would like to follow. You will be stuck in the slow lane with the other losers. That's the place where you find people whose only achievement is that the fruit of their labour may go some way towards making someone else's goals come true.

If you fail to plan, you plan to fail. It may sound trite or even a bit 'clever' when it's put like that. But it is none the less true. There is no neutral gear available and if you have no direction forward you will drift back as negatives take control.

There are two words which are coming increasingly into regular use and it is worth thinking about them so that once you understand what they imply you can make a choice as to which will best define your future. The words are REACTIVE and PROACTIVE.

The reactive person goes through life being aware of what is going on round him and when he sees what is happening he reacts to it and makes the next decision for his life and where he is going next. Let's be fair - that could be a lot worse. At least that person is making decisions.

The proactive person goes through life realising that for most of the time he can be responsible for what is going on round him. He makes things happen to his world before his world takes over to make things happen to him. His working and living pattern is based on "Today I will ..." "Tomorrow I will ..." "Next week I will ..." and so on.

Being positively REACTIVE is not going to be a disaster - at least you are going to make some decisions. But ask yourself will you be happy to have the main pattern of your life changed from day to day by decisions of others. Wouldn't you rather be saying to yourself - "This is my life and I want to be responsible for it".

As social beings belonging to an ordered society we cannot avoid the responsibilities that REACTION will bring. They will be there when the tax-bill comes in the post or when your daughter tells you you are going to be a grandparent! But why not go for the Winner's Start and make the decision that as much of your life is going to be as PROACTIVE as you can make it.

Plan daily. Remember the thirty minutes each day we have talked of allocating to yourself. That's another thing to fit in there. List the 'Things to Do' and get the satisfaction of being able to cross out yesterday's list which has become 'Things Done'.

Equally be sure to look beyond your own selfish self-interest as you plan. Particularly if you have decided to go PROACTIVE you can be sure that your plans are going to have an impact on the lives of others. People on the winning track will create winning opportunities for others without exploiting them. Losers look in. Winners look out and know that they will live every moment, enjoying, relating, doing and giving as much as they can.

Remember that it is not only good people who plan. Evil men will often realise that they need to do the same if they are going to succeed. Hitler had a clear plan which involved others around him, then his whole country and eventually much of the world. He had made his plans clear and to the defeated and downtrodden Germany of the 1920's much of what he had to say sounded attractive. He would restore national pride by national achievement. People found it easy to turn a blind eye to the rottenness of the other half of the apple. It was that great Irish philosopher Edmund Burke who said 200 years ago "The only thing necessary for the triumph of evil, is for good men to do nothing".

Apologists for the great materialistic ideology of communism often tried to point out what they saw as the common philosophy between communism and Christianity - ideas like equal shares for everybody. They ignored as unimportant, because it suited their purpose, the categorical statement by Lenin "We must remove the myth of God from the mind of man". Recent events following the upheavals in the former USSR have shown that in spite of all their efforts, what they called the 'myth of God' had extraordinary staying power.

The dangerous attraction of extremists of whatever persuasion is that they often make themselves popular in their emergent days by saying in a loud voice what many people think in their hearts but would be ashamed to say out loud on their own behalf.

Start with your winning pattern at home. When honesty steps in you may well find that it calls for change in yourself and in your closest relationships. Don't be afraid to follow the challenge. Build the winning pattern at home. 'As I am so is my family' - and that can lead by a logical expansion to 'As I am so is my nation'. You cannot demand standards of behaviour and morality for your country which you are not prepared to set for yourself.

Winners listen. They listen to other people's needs because they recognise the vital importance of the philosophy which can be summarised as **Making the Other Fellow Great.** All my life I have been fortunate in that people seemed to be prepared to talk to me about themselves and to ask me for my advice over their problems. This can have frightening responsibilities.

In the late 1960's I produced a series of television programmes in which sixth-formers had the chance of cross-questioning public figures. The youngsters brought a refreshing simplicity to the process of interview, often asking questions which were devastating because they were based on their own honesty.

I got to know some of them very well and they seemed to trust me. Jill went on to Cambridge where she had a brilliant academic career. While she was there she came back to see me and I took her up to the canteen for a cup of coffee. Suddenly she said "David, I want your advice". She had fallen in love with a fellow student and the question she asked me was should she fall in with his demands and go to bed with him! I thought as quickly as I could and answered along these lines.

"Jill, it is not for me to make that decision for you. That's up to you. But this I will say. During those months when you were making programmes with me I got to like you a lot and to respect what I believe you stand for. Whatever your decision is I will still like you just as much and I'm not going to ask you what the decision is. However if I know that you decide to go ahead and have sex with him I'm not sure that I would still respect you".

I was more than a little stunned when this gorgeous youngster leant across the canteen table and kissed me. "Thanks for being honest" she said. I never did ask her what decision she took, but I did feel that I had made a positive contribution not only to her situation but to our future relationship.

Look back on your own early life and ask yourself who influenced you most positively; it might be parents or grandparents, teacher or friend. For sure they will have been people who cared. Try to remember what that meant to you and pass it on in your turn. Avoid being over-caring. You must allow freedom of choice to those you are concerned with. They will not forgive you or value your help or advice if they feel stifled by it.

If you find that you have come up against what looks like an insuperable problem, unless it surrounds you totally, try to walk away from it for a while. Try helping others. The results of doing that may have dramatic effects on your own situation. But don't forget the Bible's warning of the mote and the beam. A friend or colleague is unlikely to be impressed by your own advice if he knows that you are being defeated on your own front in your own life.

If people feel that they are getting the best out of themselves when they are with you then the probability is that you are on the right track yourself. The best evidence that you are a winner can be seen not in your material achievements but in the joy of positive relationships. Relationships with people, relationships with God, relationships with the rest of the world.

If we get things right we will be well on the way to fulfilling our greatest responsibility to hand on a worthwhile world to the next generation. In many cases that next generation has gone ahead of us, particularly in its sense of caring for the world and our environment. We must be ready to learn from them and to make sure that if they follow our example they will not end up uncaring or without hope for the future.

We can have a very direct effect on the way we manage ourselves, on how we manage our relationships with other people and with the world. While we do so it is well to remember that we all have one asset to work with that is ultimately limited - the asset of life or time. Time flies. You can never live yesterday over again. Look at yourself and your life to date. Have you made full use of the time you have already had? If you get a negative answer, don't get too depressed. Instead make a positive decision to make more productive use of the present and the future. It doesn't take for ever to catch up.

Remember Kipling's 'unforgiving minute'. For your future look to fill each minute with 'sixty seconds' worth of distance run'. Avoid putting yourself into the position of saying "I wish I had ..." but realising it too late.

Take time and make yourself its master.

Plan your time

Time to spend with people, family, young and old.

Time to read, to work, to keep your health, to play.

Do this by taking time for yourself to plan how you will use it.

If you use just 30 minutes out of every 24 hours to plan the effective use of the rest of your time, you are getting good value for money.

In the past you may have thought "Someday I would like to do this" or "Someday I will do that". Looking back you are probably still saying "Someday".

Take your "Someday" plans and make them part of your planned goals. Use that sort of "Someday" thinking in a positive way. Use those awful unfulfilled wishes as rewards for yourself. If your dream planning and goal-setting is designed to stretch you enough and to increase your potential, you probably won't achieve everything on your list. In fact, if you keep your plans under regular revision you never should complete them all. But at the same time it is important that you don't become so obsessed with achievement (business or material success or whatever) that you don't have time to enjoy the fruits. So plan some of those presently unfulfilled 'Someday' wishes into your goal pattern.

For example if one of your plans is to increase your business turnover by 25% in the next year - add the rider - and **when (NB - not If)** when I achieve that target I'm going to fly Concorde to New York to visit my brother.

The 'Someday' dream has become part of the planned pattern. The happiness you have imagined and planned has become something really experienced in real time and not in the far distant country of your imagination.

People often put things off because they are afraid of failure. But that is not always the whole truth. There is another motive which is not so easy to identify or to admit. The fear of success is not easy to acknowledge. And yet we know that the consequences of making a positive decision will often be new responsibilities which we are either too afraid or too selfish to face up to. And so the decision becomes another 'Someday' thing.

Winners don't work like that or think like that. They take the first step forward in faith with accepted goals that give their future lives the richness of a true purpose.

In each section there has been a reminder check list to help underline what has been said.

As you make your decision to be a winner use this list to check on your situation.

1) How do I fit into my family, my work, my community, my nation?

2) Remember to tell those you love that it's true - every day.

3) If the children are still at home give them special time today and every day.

4) Contact someone specially to tell them that they matter in your life.

5) Do something constructive that you know will not produce any pay-off or obligation.

6) Do something special this weekend for yourself. Repeat this at least once a month.

7) What are your goals for your lifetime? Write down what you would like your children to tell people about you.

8) Make out a game plan for goals in all aspects of your life. Write down one to be achieved in the next 5 years in each of the following

Career	Financial
Physical condition	You in the community
Family	Educational
Personal Attitude	Entertainment

9) Remember your daily personal allocation of 30 minutes to yourself is going to prove the time of your life.

* * * * *

So that's the end - or hopefully for you it may prove to be the beginning. The decision is waiting to be made. The person to make it can only be you.

Appendix 1

Shakespeare's Advice To A Young Man

Polonius' speech to Laertes

And these few precepts in thy memory
Look thou character. Give thy thoughts no tongue,
Nor any unproportion'd thought his act.
Be thou familiar, but by no means vulgar;
The friends thou hast, and their adoption tried,
Grapple them to thy soul with hoops of steel;
But do not dull thy palm with entertainment
Of each new-hatch'd, unfledg'd comrade. Beware
Of entrance to a quarrel; but, being in,
Bear't that th' opposed may beware of thee.
Give every man thine ear, but few thy voice;
Take each man's censure, but reserve thy judgment.
Costly thy habit as thy purse can buy,
But not express'd in fancy; rich, not gaudy;
For the apparel oft proclaims the man,
And they in France of the best rank and station
Are most select and generous, chief in that.
Neither a borrower, nor a lender be;
For loan oft loses both itself and friend,
And borrowing dulls the edge of husbandry,
This above all; to thine own self be true,
And it must follow, as the night the day,
Thou canst not then be false to any man.

Appendix 2

Rudyard Kipling's Advice To A Young Man

'IF'

If you can keep your head when all about you
Are losing theirs and blaming it on you;
If you can trust yourself when all men doubt you,
But make allowance for their doubting too;
If you can wait and not be tired by waiting,
Or being lied about, don't deal in lies,
Or being hated, don't give way to hating,
And yet don't look too good, nor talk too wise;
If you can dream - and not make dreams your master,
If you can think - and not make thoughts your aim,
If you can meet with Triumph and Disaster
And treat those two imposters just the same...

If you can make one heap of all your winnings
And risk it on one turn of pitch-and-toss,
And lose, and start again at your beginnings
And never breathe a word about your loss...

If you can talk with crowds and keep your virtue,
Or walk with Kings - nor lose the common touch,
If neither foes nor loving friends can hurt you,
If all men count with you, but none too much;
If you can fill the unforgiving minute
With sixty second's worth of distance run,
Yours is the Earth and everything that's in it,
And - which is more - you'll be a Man, my son!